HIL
f

The Cinematic Theater

Babak A. Ebrahimian

The Scarecrow Press, Inc.
Lanham, Maryland • Toronto • Oxford
2004

SCARECROW PRESS, INC.

Published in the United States of America
by Scarecrow Press, Inc.
A wholly owned subsidiary of
The Rowman & Littlefield Publishing Group, Inc.
4501 Forbes Boulevard, Suite 200, Lanham, Maryland 20706
www.scarecrowpress.com

PO Box 317
Oxford
OX2 9RU, UK

British Library Cataloguing in Publication Information Available

Library of Congress Cataloging-in-Publication Data

Ebrahimian, Babak A.
  The cinematic theater / Babak A. Ebrahimian.
    p. cm.
  Includes bibliographical references and index.
  ISBN 0-8108-4987-9 (pbk. : alk. paper)
  1. Motion pictures and theater. I. Title.
PN1995.25.E27 2004
791.43—dc22
                                    2004007084

To the first four in my life:
Violette, Mehdi, Leila, and Luigi

Contents

List of Figures

Foreword

There have been quite a number of writers and directors in the modernist and postmodern period that attempted to devise a model for the theater's future aesthetics. Several of them also created performances they staged in ways that would demonstrate the potential as well as the implications of their theatrical vision. Names such as Antonin Artaud, Bertolt Brecht, Peter Brook, and Jerzy Grotowski, among others, may come to mind.

In this book, Babak Ebrahimian tells us about a very recent example of such a project, namely the evolution of a model that he named the "Cinematic Theater." It is an ambitious effort to analyze and theorize the sources as well as the practice of what might constitute a theater, which would be performed on stage, yet employ selected aesthetics of film.

A particularly important aspect of Ebrahimian's study is the detailed description the performances he was able to stage with a deeply committed group of performers—a collective, as one might call it—who were inspired by his desire for exploring the major influences that shaped Western theater during the later 20th century.

Many of these developments have been subsumed under categories such as "postmodern theater" or "post-dramatic theater." Ebrahimian's book recounts his experimentation with a variety of texts and staging practices during the years when he collaborated with actors who shared his curiosity and stubborn insistence to query the validity of contemporary performance modes and their use-value for the theater of our time.

There has been no want of analytical and interpretative efforts trying to define what would constitute a postmodern theater. Bonnie Marranca's book *The Theatre of Images*, comes to mind, of course, along with notions such as *theater as landscape, theater of the body, nonnarrative theater, multimedia theater,* and others that tried to capture various aspects of recent theatrical invention.

Ebrahimian's wrestling with the concept of a cinematic stage is a comparable effort of evolving a model for the present and future practice of live theater. It draws its strength from aligning contemporary film theory with the conceptualization of a postmodern performance mode. What makes his approach especially valuable is the extensive testing in performance with the "Experimental Theater Lab" (in short: ETL), the ensemble he assembled while completing his graduate studies at Stanford.

I had occasion to watch much of the company's work, in rehearsal as well as in public showings, and was intrigued by the intensity and scope of the experimentation the group conducted. Their experiments resulted frequently in compelling performances but did also, at times, lead to a dead end. The latter experience, however, offered them invaluable insights that facilitated fresh approaches they would employ in subsequent projects. ETL's rehearsal and performance practice yielded the solid foundation Ebrahimian could build on when he endeavored to theorize his model of a cinematic theater. His knowledge of the aesthetics of film, its history, and theory, provided the other base, which helped in the development of his concept. The third pillar—if one might call it that—was constructed from his close scrutiny of experimental contemporary theater, as he witnessed it in the work of Pina Bausch, Richard Foreman, Heiner Müller, Peter Stein, Robert Wilson, and other proponents of a postmodern theater. In this case, again, it was not only performances he watched but also the rehearsals he was permitted to observe, that enriched his understanding of the space/time dimension that makes live performance so different and, one might argue, much more compelling than the recorded two-dimensional image we are watching on the screen.

Babak Ebrahimian's book will certainly provoke debate and, as I hope, productive discussions about the potential of the cinematic stage where a new mode of presentation would merge features of live and of recorded performance, and thus create a cinematic theater. As it has happened with other manifestos, which undertook it in their own moment to map the landscape of the theater's future, impulses set in motion by this book might greatly contribute to the shape of performance, as we will witness it in the years to come.

Carl Weber
Stanford University

Preface

This book is the product of an exploration in theater and film spanning a period of fifteen years. Director or observer, I have always regarded theater and film as two sibling art forms. Although my work as a director has primarily focused on the theater, since a young age I have been fascinated by cinema. The great film directors have been as much of an inspiration and grounding for me as have great theater directors. In many ways, I can say the cinema was my first love. With these two art forms at the center of my artistic and intellectual interest, my pursuit to understand the theater through cinema was a natural one. The two art forms have much in common: they share questions of aesthetics, the art of story-telling, the ability to address historical, humanistic, social, and political issues, some overlapping history, and a collaborative and ensemble process.

Despite their similarities, theater and film remain autonomous in their forms. Why is this the case? What makes them so independent of one another? Could a shared aesthetic and form be possible, and if so, what would it be? How would it look and sound? Could the theater look and "behave" more like the cinema, and what new possibilities would this open up? As early as 1989, these questions started my search for a "cinematic theater." Looking at the stage before me, I wished I could have a live film on it.

This book documents the theories, process, and results that led me to develop and define the cinematic theater. This work included experimentation and explorations with the epic theater and the cinematic form, and an examination of the theater stage, space, and design. Both theoretical and practical explorations have been crucial parts of this process. To fully understand the nature of both art forms and how they could work together, I needed to direct theater and films in a systematic and experimental manner before I could formulate a cinematic aesthetic and form for the theater.

Anyone who has ever been part of a theater or film production will tell you that both art forms require the participation and assistance of many people. Hundreds of hands join to create a theater or film production. In the light of this complexity, it is simply impossible for me to name all those who have helped and collaborated to make these productions a reality. There are, however, some whose help and guidance along the way hold a definite and special place.

In 1989, I assisted Liviu Ciulei at New York University's Tisch School of the Arts. Liviu is an accomplished theater and film director, and also a trained architect who designed many of his own sets. In working with him, I not only learned about many facets and details of the theater, but also had the opportunity to engage him in a rich dialogue about films. If anyone is equipped to assess the differences and similarities between film and theater, it is Liviu. I am thankful for his friendship and support, and my appreciation for him and his wife, Helga, continue to this day.

In 1990, I began my graduate studies at Stanford University, where I met and began working with Carl Weber, a former assistant and collaborator of Bertolt Brecht. Carl is an extremely precise teacher, artist, and intellectual, and it was while working with him that I quickly learned to do away with generalities and focus on details. Carl has been a voice of support, challenge, and refinement of the cinematic theater since its inception. More recently, I also owe Carl much thanks for his feedback on the manuscript. I am forever grateful to Carl and his wife Marianne for their friendship and support.

I cannot but thank the core ensemble members of the Experimental Theater Lab (ETL), who inspired and worked with me throughout the most significant elements of this exploration. They include: Michael Nichols, Kaki Bernard, Cynthia Wong, Joshua Correll, Matthew Getz, Jessica Bar, Eva Bunker, and Andrey Ustinov. Hamid Arjomand contributed significantly as a designer and key collaborator. Julie Kuhlken assistant-directed numerous productions. Without the sincere dedication of these core ensemble members, there would have been no productions, no definition, and no practical evidence for the theory.

I would like to thank Andrea McConnaha for her invaluable assistance on my film projects, especially *The Last Goodbye* (1997). Harrigan MacMahon read and offered valuable feedback on several chapters of the manuscript during an independent study on Werner Herzog and Wim Wenders at Columbia University in 2002.

While developing the theoretical grounding for the cinematic theater at Stanford University, René Girard provided a valuable critical examination of this work in its original form, *Time-Space Transfiguration and the Unfolding of the [Frame]*. Marjorie Perloff offered encouragement on this project, as well as intellectual challenges regarding aesthetics and the postmodern. Hans Ulrich Gumbrecht and Jean-Pierre Dupuy, also of Stanford University, and Anne Berger of Cornell University, have been of great support. Bruce Smith, Kathy Eden and Hamid Dabashi of Columbia University have provided invaluable feedback and encouragement. The support and challenges of such scholars have no doubt contributed to a more comprehensible manuscript. In addition, I am grateful to Richard Foreman and Heiner Müller (1929–1995) for their time and valuable insights, many of which are found in this book.

Three friends to whom I owe thanks are James Schaefer, Allen Zadoff, and John Zucker for their engagement in various parts of the process. In more recent years, I would like to thank Rebecca and Bruce Conrad for their help and sustained interest. Stephen Ryan and Karen Gray of Scarecrow Press have been extraordinarily kind and helpful throughout the process of finalizing and editing this book. It goes without saying that one's family can be the greatest support. This indeed has been my case, for which I am most grateful. They have witnessed my journey from the start, and have helped see me through its ups and downs. I would particularly like to thank my siblings, Laleh and David, for their unfailing help and love on my film and theater projects. I owe immense thanks, to which words cannot do justice, to my beloved wife, Esther, who has been more than understanding, cheerful, and strong throughout. Her support on various theater and film projects has been constant and unending, and her patient help on the manuscript has enabled this book to take a smooth route towards its final form. My thanks to her could take pages, though I hope the filled stages to come can better express my gratitude.

Introduction
The Cinematic Theater: Time–Space Transfiguration of the Theater Stage

I still cannot forget that work of a genius, shown in the last century, the film with which it all started—*L'Arrivée d'un Train en Gare de la Ciotate*. The film made by August Lumière was simply the result of the invention of the camera, the film, and the projector. The spectacle which only lasts half a minute, shows a section of railway platform, bathed in sunlight, ladies and gentlemen walking about, and the train coming from the depths of a frame and heading straight for the camera. As the train approached panic started in the theater: people jumped up and ran away. That was the moment when cinema was born; it was not simply a question of technique, or just a new way of reproducing the world. What came into being was a new aesthetic principle.

—Andrey Tarkovsky[1]

The panic that Tarkovsky speaks of here has yet not quieted down. It is the panic of cinema; the panic of people standing in lines for hours in order to get a blockbuster movie ticket; of Academy Awards, who is there, and who wears what; it is the panic induced by film festivals and the glamour of the whole industry taking over humans' desires; it is the panic of, "imitate us, we are the movie 'stars'."

The arrival of the train in that short and "insignificant" film caused a moment of panic, inducing the audience to run away from the train—that is, from the moving image on the screen. Today's panic is the reverse motion: the audience runs toward the movie houses and waits for hours merely to obtain tickets. Then, the panic was with a scream, today's panic is with a screen of "thrills," giving birth to the "thrillers." Tarkovsky notes that the panic and screams of 1895 were not without product. They gave birth to cinema, and the cinema was just not just a technique or "a new way of reproducing the world," it was also a new era for art, bringing with it a "new aesthetic principle."

1

Since the invention of cinema in 1895, almost all the arts and the entertainment industries have, in one shape or another, undergone both basic as well as significant transformations. Influenced by the cinema and its technology, popular culture has not only been affected in its aesthetics but also in its content. Culture has also appropriated film when and where possible: from music, as seen and heard, for example, on MTV, to poetry, novels, comic books, paintings, sculptures, dance, design, and art installations. Traces of the cinema and the screen image can be found at work not only on the local street, but also in a global context throughout the world in an emerging global culture.

Significant or not, cinema's influence has become part of our daily audio, visual, and verbal vocabulary. Screen "stars" have become screen icons: Humphrey Bogart, Ingrid Bergman, James Dean, and Marilyn Monroe, for example, are now commonplace images, printed on t-shirts, photographs, and art prints. In addition, another 20th century invention has come to the aid of the cinema industry: the television. According to UNESCO, in 1995, 805 out of one thousand households in the United States had a television, and even in developing countries, they are spreading rapidly.[2] Films are now seen directly on the television via television channels, cable, satellite dish, videotapes, or the more contemporary technologies of the DVD. Reflecting on the globalization of culture through television, the German playwright Heiner Müller once remarked, "Even the slums of Brazil have television antennas."[3] With such a wide reach via the large screen of the movie houses or the small screen of the television, films and cinema "stars" have also become models for imitation, from fashion to even politics, from children to adults, and among the rich and the poor.[4] The cinema has become, both as a form of communication as well as a form of art, a high-impact, global industry, gaining recognition and influence throughout the world.

The theater[5]—a nearly three thousand-year-old art form that uses poetry (written and spoken text), as well as movement, sound, and other elements such as costume and scenery—has also been influenced and changed by cinema and its advances in modern technology. As early as the 1920s, the German theater director Erwin Piscator, known primarily for his political theater, was already at work, experimenting with films on his stage. His famous production of *Rasputin, The Romanovs, The War and The People That Rose Against Them* (1927), used a variety of theatrically sophisticated elements, including a revolving hemisphere in which the opening sequences of scenes were staged simultaneously with a documentary montage of text, photos, and sounds. Additionally, film segments were projected and incorporated into the action.

Though the technical aspects of the production were ultimately too expensive to make this visionary's production possible, *Rasputin* influenced and inspired another young playwright and director: the thirty-year-old Bertolt Brecht. Brecht was now to carry on with the experiments and formulate the theory of "Epic Theater." Following Piscator and Brecht—who was also influenced by the cinema both in theory as well as in practice, and greatly admired screen figures such as Charlie Chaplin—continued with the exploration of bringing film onto the stage. A particularly memorable usage of the film on the theater stage is his production of *The Mother* (1951), in which film projection was used in the final scene to emphasize the closure of the play. With the arrival of the cinema, as early as the 1920s, theater did not remain untouched. Consciously or not, the theater carried on to explore and exchange with the cinema.

Today, as two distinct art forms, cinema and theater still maintain an ongoing dialogue with one another. A play is sometimes made into a film and similarly, a screenplay is sometimes adapted for the stage. Examples of such adaptations and exchanges of contents between the stage and screen, and vice versa, are far too many to enumerate, though an example of one such well-known classic exchange would be *A Streetcar Named Desire*, written by Tennessee Williams and directed by Elia Kazan.[6]

Though not as prominent and visible, the influence of film form and aesthetics can be detected in a few contemporary theaters and theaters companies. The Wooster Group, one of the leading avant-garde companies in the country, for example, almost always uses video monitors and film segments in its staging of plays—be they classical texts (staged in a deconstructed/reconstructed manner) or original pieces. The usage of the live video projection and video monitors is further accentuated and accompanied by microphones and other advanced audiovisual technology.

With a common history of over 100 years, various intersections, and a rich legacy of interaction, it is clear that theater and cinema are not far from one another, but are rather positioned at different formal intersections. They have been in dialogue and in active exchange with one another. Yet, the theater has still not fully embraced the cinema and adopted a truly cinematic approach to its stage.

Despite all its innovations and radical departures since the turn of the 20th century, and despite significant intersections, the theater has not yet fully pushed its boundaries to maximize the advantages offered by cinema, or the "moving image." After all, the "moving image" is what occurs on the theater stage and is also another name for the cinema: "motion picture." To create a more cinematic image for the theater and the theater space—to shift form from a "moving image" to a "motion picture"—it becomes necessary to examine the differences and similarities between the two forms of art: theater and cinema.

The most obvious difference between theater and cinema is their immediacy. Theater's essence is located in its *presence*, whereas cinema's essence is located in its *distancing*. The actor seen on stage is alive, utters speech, and moves around on stage, and as the play unfolds and movements take place, the audience witnesses it. There is direct synchronicity between the time of the stage and that of the audience watching it.

In the two opening lines of his book *The Empty Space* (1968), Brook defines theater in its broadest sense as follows: "I can take any empty space and call it a bare stage. A man walks across this empty space whilst someone else is watching him, and this is all that is needed for an act of theater to be engaged."[7] According to this definition, then, the three elements required to create and define the theatre are: a stage (a three-dimensional, or R3, space),[8] a body (the actor), and a spectator (the audience). [9] These three are located together in the present time.

Film, on the other hand, has its essence located in *distance*—or in the past—in an *absence*. A film that is projected on a screen (R2) could have been made yesterday, a year ago, or a decade ago. In this manner, the film is distanced in time. Furthermore, the film is being projected onto the screen by an apparatus at the end of the "movie theater" space: there lies an additional spatial distancing. In watching a film, nothing is based on presence except the actual act of projection. "A film, or a scene, is shot," the film director would say, then it is left behind until the editing process. After the editing process, the *montage*, is completed, the film is ready to be presented, and projected for the audience.

Liviu Ciulei, former artistic director of the Guthrie Theater in Minneapolis and winner of the prize for best director at the Cannes Film Festival for *The Forest of the Hanged* (1965), remarks on the difference between directing theater and films:

> In the theater, the director must have his concepts in mind the whole time, and must share it with his collaborators. They must all converge to obtain the results he wants. In film, the result exists only in the mind of the director—and even if he wants to share it, I doubt he can really do it. It's a very solitary kind of work: he is alone. He can only express in shots and sequences. But the collaborators will seldom understand the vision before seeing the result. Film is completely a fragmentary process.[10]

In films, the scene is usually rehearsed once or twice, and then it is filmed in several takes. Once the scene is filmed, the director moves on. Unlike the theater, there is no room for the scene to grow, develop, and acquire its own life. The filming process can even begin with the last scene filmed first. With scene after scene filmed, sequence after sequence completed, fragments of the entire film are completed, and the final product is brought to a completion in the editing process.

In the theater, on the other hand, the scene is rehearsed over and over again, and every time it is rehearsed, it is developed further. Contrary to the cinema, where a scene is filmed many times and the best "take" is chosen during the editing phase, the process of rehearsal in the theater contributes to and is a large part of theater's immediacy and life on stage. The scene can be rehearsed over and over again until performance night. And even then, subtle changes and improvements can be made depending on the audience reaction or a new discovery. The following anecdote illustrates the importance and immediacy in the theater:

I did a play with that perfectionist Alfred Lunt. In the first act, he had a scene sitting on a bench. In rehearsal, he suggested, as a piece of natural business, taking his shoe off and rubbing his foot. Then he added shaking the shoe to empty it before putting it back on again. One day when we were on tour in Boston, I walked past his dressing room. The door was ajar. He was preparing for the performance, but I could see that he was looking out for me. He beckoned excitedly, I went into the dressing room, he closed the door, asked me to sit down. 'There is something I want to try tonight,' he said. 'But only if you agree. I went for a walk on Boston Common this afternoon and found these.' He held out his palm. It contained two tiny pebbles. 'That scene where I shake out my shoe,' he continued, 'it's always worried me that nothing falls out. So I thought I'd try putting the pebbles in. Then when I shake it, you'd see them drop—and you'd hear the sound. What do you think?' I said it was an excellent idea and his face lit up. He looked delightedly at the two little stones, back at me, then suddenly his expression changed. He studied the stones again for a long anxious moment. 'You don't think it would be better with one?'[11]

It appears that one pebble or two should not make a difference, and yet, for the perfectionist, Alfred Lunt, it made enough of a difference to ask the director for his suggestion, and after the production had opened and was on tour. Theater is located in the present time, where actors perform and audiences watch, and should one small detail enhance the performance or the production, unlike the released film, it can be added.

This immediacy in theater and the lack of it in the cinema is echoed by the director/critic Robert Brustein. In comparing the theater to the cinema, he writes:

> If the theatre has a single advantage over film and television it is its immediacy. Dramatic events exist in a continuum of present time, while celluloid and videotape, no matter how convincing or realistic the photography, are imprisoned in the past (so is narrative fiction, which declares its past condition with the author's "he saids" and "she saids"). The media are not happening; they have already happened. We are witnesses of history, remote, aloof, involuntarily disengaged.[12]

For Brustein, as for Brook and other theater (and for that matter "stage") critics, writers, and directors alike, theater's essence and uniqueness lies in the fact that it is occurring in the "here and now," defying the past and being in the present. In this light, theater as an art form is rooted in the present time, privileging presence over distancing or absence. It has a *presence*: *it presents, it narrates, it engages*, and constantly remains in the present time—the present moment. Using this fact, Brook also points out the difference between cinema and theater both temporally as well as spatially:

> There is only one interesting difference between cinema and the theatre. The cinema flashes on to a screen images from the past. As this is what the mind

does to itself all through life, the cinema seems intimately real. Of course, it is nothing of the sort—it is a satisfying and enjoyable extension of the unreality of everyday perception. The theatre, on the other hand, always asserts itself in the present. This is what can make it more real than the normal stream of consciousness.[13]

The theater is based on presence, whereas the cinema is based on distancing, in time as well as space. The difference spoken of here also alludes to the fact that the cinema is an art form that is completely dependent on technology. "Flashes on to a screen" and "images from the past" both imply technology. Capturing the present and repeating it again and again requires not only a camera that can frame and capture the instances—for a motion picture is composed of a series of instances projected seen one after the other—but also requires a variety of technologies, including microphones, recorders, lights, a projector, and ultimately a dark house with a screen, the so-called "movie theater." Without these elements, experiencing—seeing and hearing—an image from the past in the present moment would not be possible.

In discussing, and even defending, the nature of time in the cinema, Andrey Tarkovsky writes:

> Time is said to be irreversible. And this is true enough in the sense that 'you can't bring back the past', as they say. But what exactly is this 'past'? Is it what has passed? And what does "passed" mean for a person for when for each of us the past is the bearer of all that is constant in the reality of the present, of each current moment? In a certain sense the past is far more real, or at any rate more stable, more resilient than the present. The present slips and vanishes like sand between the fingers, acquiring material weight only in its recollection.[14]

Examining the primary similarities and differences of the theater and the cinema, one first finds that the spatial elements in both forms differ from one another. In the theater, the space is a three-dimensional (R3) one, whereas in the cinema—despite its portrayal of a three-dimensional world—a screen is used, and, therefore, a two-dimensional space (R2) is at work within the three-dimensional "movie house." Time in the theater is a variable (V); from production to production it varies; it can be controlled—prolonged or shortened—whereas in cinema, the time of a film is fixed. The performance in the theater is immediate and takes place in the present (I); in the cinema, as discussed, the performance is recorded and projected, and, thereby, it is distanced (D) in both time and space. The same can also be said of the element of sound for most theater productions; it is immediate, whereas in the cinema, as with the image, it is recorded and played back in time in synchronicity with the projected image, and is thereby also distanced (D). These differences can be mapped out as follows:

	THEATER	FILM
SPACE	stage (R3): I	screen (R3 on R2): D
TIME	variable: V	fixed: constant C
ACTORS	immediate: I	filmed: D
SOUND	immediate: I	recorded: D

The question that remains to be answered is: How can these aesthetic differences in form be reconciled to enable the theater stage to expand into a cinematic one, and to define the *cinematic image* for the theater? This shift and transfiguration of the theater's time and space becomes the basic definition of the *cinematic theater*.

On a more formal level, the *cinematic theater* can be defined as "a theater that has a cinematic (film) form and structure, and functions (operates) as if it were a film." It is a theater with a film form, or in other words, it is a stage that looks, sounds, and behaves like the cinema: a theater with a so-called *cinematic stage*. Behind this definition, two primary theoretical principles govern and define its form and structure: (i) montage theory, as first defined and developed by Sergei Eisenstein, and (ii) spatial and perceptual distancing (vs. the Brechtian distancing). Without eradicating the theater's essence—the immediate life that it has on stage—these two principles, when applied to the theater space, redefine and reinterpret the theatrical stage according to the cinematic form, thereby enabling and defining the *cinematic theater*.

Applying the first principle, montage, yields a fragmented narrative structure. Here, the text transforms itself into a fragmented sequence where every scene becomes a tableau that can stand on its own, independent of the other scenes, and can have its autonomous self-contained pregnant moment. Comparable to Brecht's epic theater, montage theory goes a step further in that it allows multiple sequences of narrative to share the same time.

The second principle redefines and reconfigures the stage by "screening" and distancing its elements. Not all elements can be distanced, however, as the essence of theater, after all, is its immediacy: it takes place in the present time. For the cinematic theater, on the other hand, distancing plays an important role, as this is a large part and definition (not to mention difference with theater) of the cinema and the cinematic form. The following table shows how the cinematic theater combines the elements of the two forms:

	CINEMATIC THEATER
SPACE	framed, screened, and distanced stage: R3 distanced
TIME	fixed: constant C
ACTORS	immediate, but screened and distanced
SOUND	recorded: D

Beyond the two principles described and illustrated previously, the cinematic theater defines a constant time for the performance through the principle of *vertical montage*. There is no possibility of a play's run varying in duration. Just as in the cinema, time becomes a constant: it is fixed. As a consequence, all stage elements—text, sound, music, movement, and image—can appear side by side and with an equal degree of importance. Within such a transfigured stage, the theater becomes a site where it can stage and display any play, classical or contemporary, in a cinematic manner: on a cinematic stage of a cinematic theater. This book demonstrates the formulation and definition of the cinematic theater, both in theory and practice. It is structured as follows.

Chapter 1, Precursors to the Cinematic Theater, predominantly examines the role of images in contemporary culture and theater. The first section looks at the notion of the *hyperreal*, as defined by Jean Baudrillard, and its role in today's culture and images. In the second and the third sections, focus will be given to two figures of the late American avant-garde theater, whose works are highly image-based: Robert Wilson and Richard Foreman. Looking at how these two theater writer-directors (auteurs) stage their texts for their theater work, this chapter then lays the groundwork for the remaining chapters, addressing the issue of how the theater can shift from a "stage image" to a "cinematic image" on its stage and in its space.

Chapter 2, Space and Structure, defines the space and structure of the cinematic theater. The chapter begins by examining how the two physical spaces of cinema and theater differ and how the theater space can be transformed into a cinematic one. The principles and theories used for this transformation include Bentham's *Panopticon* and the *panoptic space*; Peter Eisenman's architectural notion of the *fold*, which for the theater space translates as a *frame with a screen*; and finally the German set design notion of *Raum*, or room/space. Together, when applied to the theater space, these three principles transform the space into that of a cinematic theater. What inhabits this space is then the narrative.

The latter half of this chapter examines the narrative structure of the cinema and the epic theater. The two structures are similar in that they both frame the narrative into a *tableau*—each frame contains one image, and together, "frame + image," they create the tableau. The tableaux are each well defined and precisely constructed so as to give the audience full information and pleasure. The narrative is constructed and presented to the viewer through a sequencing of these tableaux—through a montage of tableaux or "attractions."

Chapter 3, Sequencing in Time, focuses entirely on the theory of montage. The theory, as first developed and formally articulated by Sergei M. Eisenstein, contains two distinct parts: (i) *montage of attractions* and (ii) *vertical montage*. Montage of attractions is a theory for the visual track of the film based on the sequencing of the tableaux. More commonly referred to as montage, it explains the construction of the narrative through the sequencing of framed images (the tableaux). The second form of montage, called vertical montage, theorizes the one-to-one correlation and relationship between sound and the montage of attractions, or the sequence of tableaux. The vertical montage also establishes a fixed correspondence between the visual track and the soundtrack, thus creating a closed system for the cinematic frame. Each discussion of the montage form includes a subsection titled "application," which gives the implications and concrete examples of the montage theory.

Chapter 4, Unfolding the [Framed Theater]: The Cinematic Theater, begins by examining how both forms of montage can be applied to the cinema. This is done through a close analysis of Orson Welles' 1941 film, *Citizen Kane*. Though the script of *Citizen Kane* is highly dependent on montage, Welles manages to create a new form for the cinema by doing away with montage and replacing it with a frame, or a fixed camera. By placing the camera at a fixed point of view and shooting with a depth of field, Welles filmed entire scenes in one tableau. In this way, Welles does away with the montage of attractions and thereby creates a [framed theater]: "framed" by the camera and "theater" because it is a complete tableaux, a complete theater scene—without any division or cutting—viewed, or [framed], through the camera. In creating the [framed theater], the vertical montage plays a crucial role. While it continues to link the audio to the visual, as demonstrated, it also functions as a plane of focus.

Following the analysis and definition of the [framed theater], the second half of Chapter 4 demonstrates and defines the *cinematic stage* as the unfolding of the [framed theater] on the stage. This unfolding carries out the complete application of the montage theory to the theater stage thereby transfiguring it and creating a cinematic stage. Theoretical definitions of both cinematic theater and the cinematic stage are also given at the end of this section.

Chapter 4 also concludes with an "application" section in which six explorations of the cinematic theater are presented. The section demonstrates some of the pivotal aspects of the cinematic theater and the cinematic stage that were explored through the Experimental Theater Lab (ETL) ensemble.[15] The explorations highlight and illustrate the central notions in the definition and theory of the cinematic theater.

This book defines the cinematic theater as a theater of images, sound, and technology highly appropriate for the twenty-first century—a century in which images and technology predominate. Theater can exist without any technological help. As Brook points out in his definition of theatre, all it takes to create an act of theater is a stage, an actor, and an audience. However, theater is also capable of moving in new directions. It is in this spirit that this book was written, with the hope of encouraging theater directors to take a leap forward. By combining sounds and images in their full potential, the theater will go beyond its current limits, creating a new form for new times: the cinematic theater.

10 Introduction

Notes

1. Andrey Tarkovsky, "Imprinted Time," in *Sculpting in Time*, trans. Kitty Hunter-Blair (Austin, Tex.: University of Texas Press, 1998), 62.

2. United Nations Educational, Scientific and Cultural Organization, *World Culture Report 1998: Culture, Creativity and Markets* (Paris: UNESCO Publishing), part 7, http://www.unesco.org/culture/worldreport/html_eng/graph2.shtml#a (14 September 2003).

3. Heiner Müller, in discussion with the author, May 1991.

4. For example, Ronald Reagan, who began his career as an actor in Hollywood, was elected the U.S. president for two terms (1980–1988).

5. Due to its "temporal" nature as well as its various components, theater requires a much more complicated "apparatus."

6. Today in Europe, particularly in Germany, a popular and successful trend has emerged in which well-respected directors, such as Kastorf, are staging screenplays in the theater: *Trainspotting* and *Final Destination: America* are two highly acclaimed productions.

7. Peter Brook, *The Empty Space* (New York: Atheneum, 1968), 9.

8. In mathematics, (R) is a notion designating space: (R2) is a two-dimensional space, such as a plane; (R3) is a three-dimensional space, such as a box. Beyond (R3) (i.e.,(R4) to (Rn) [n = infinity]) spaces do not exist in our perception.

9. This holds equally true for dance, the circus, comedy improvisation, and other live performance arts requiring a stage, performers, and an audience.

10. Liviu Ciulei, in discussion with the author, New York 1995.

11. Brook, *The Empty Space*, 116.

12. Robert Brustein, *Who Needs Theatre: Dramatic Opinions* (New York: Atlantic Monthly Press, 1987), 3–4.

13. Brook, *The Empty Space*, 99.

14. Tarkovsky, *Sculpting in Time*, 58.

15. The Experimental Theater Lab (ETL) was a small ensemble of actors and designers composed of American and international undergraduate and graduate students. Beginning in the fall of 1990, it was formed and developed at Stanford University. The six explorations included in this book were conceived and performed at Stanford during the years of 1990–1993, with the exception of *Michi's Blood,* which took place in New York City.

Chapter 1
Precursors to the Cinematic Theater

Images are fragile. Most of the time words don't translate them well, and when they have carried the image to the other side the emotion has all run out of it. Writing has to be careful with (E)*motion pictures.*

—Wim Wenders[1]

Real Images

Images: what we see in everyday life.

Images: We see them when we cross the street; people moving along on the sidewalk; people talking to one another; the traffic light changing from red to green; trees, buildings, and much more. Images are also observed on the signs that tell us what to wear or what to buy. Images also flash rapidly on the television screen, be they commercials or MTV. Images are also what we capture instantly with our cameras. Images are today's language, but they are also the language of theater and cinema; they are also what we see on stage, or on the screen of movie houses.

What we see during a road trip[2] is a moving picture. One perceives a window as a frame, and through this frame ones sees the images that move at the speed of the vehicle. During a trip across the United States, Jean Baudrillard observed that: "The unfolding of the desert is infinitely close to the timelessness of a film . . ."[3] Images unfolding and moving, one after another, define cinema.[4]

In his journey across America, Baudrillard discovered that much of what he saw, the contemporary landscapes and cities, functioned as a *simulacrum*—a replacement of reality with an alternative image suggesting what reality is or should look like. Sometimes, however, the images he saw—places, people, cars—appeared to be more real than the real, in other words, *hyperreal.*[5] The simulacrum and the hyperreal are not "real," nor are they "realistic." However, in their artificial way, by merely suggesting and indicating "what the real should

look like" and "how it should be," they take the place of the "real," appearing
even more realistic than the real.

Looking at Salt Lake City, Baudrillard observes: "The Christ-topped dome
(all the Christs here are copied from Thorwaldsen's and look like Bijan Borg)
straight out of *Close Encounters*: religion as special effects. In fact the whole
city has the transparency and supernatural. Other worldly cleanness of a thing
from outer space. A symmetrical, luminous, overpowering abstraction."[6] The
quality of the seen images somehow surpasses one's highest expectations. They
are clean with a "cleanness of a thing from outer space," and almost perfect with
"symmetrical, luminous overpowering abstraction." With the hyperreal, nothing—no reality—looks normal. Everything is better, greater, and closer to perfection than the norm. Even the lake, Baudrillard points out, appears to be more
real: ". . . In the heat of the desert, alongside this leaden lake, its waters also
hyperreal from sheer density of salt."[7]

Baudrillard wrote about his journey, alluding to films, cinema, and the television:

> I went in search of *astral* America, not social and cultural America, but the
> America of the empty, absolute freedom of the freeways, not the deep America
> of mores and mentalities, but the America of desert speed, of motels and sur-
> faces. I looked for it in the speed of the screenplay, in the indifferent reflex of
> television, in the films of days and nights projected across an empty space, in
> the marvelously affectless succession of signs, images, faces, and ritual acts on
> the road; looked for what was nearest to the nuclear and enucleated universe, a
> universe which is virtually our own, right down to its European cottages.[8]

Translated from the French, "l'Amérique sidérale" becomes "Astral America," but the term can also be translated as "sidereal America." The road trip
through the "astral" (the "sidereal") spaces and landscapes, filtered by Baudrillard's ability to see images in their hyperreal form, act as a film of America.

Looking at New York, Baudrillard describes an image in which "A blue-
green lorry with gleaming chromework is going down Seventh Avenue in the
early morning sun, just after a snowfall. It bears on its sides, in gold metallic
lettering, the words 'Mystic Transportation'."[9] A serene and peaceful image:
empty streets at sunrise and snowfall with a single lorry going down the avenue—a close to "perfect" image—it is brought back into reality, by the typical
"very real" inscription in "gold metallic lettering." With this small detail of a
"gleaming chromework" and "gold metallic lettering" juxtaposed with "early
morning sun, just after a snowfall" the image shifts to the hyperreal. Though for
a moment, Baudrillard likens the image to a mystic tableau—a mystic moment—he nevertheless rapidly snaps the hyperreal image back into reality by
linking it with decadence, the decadence that so strongly prevails in the non-
shiny, non-brilliant, nonmystical reality. Commenting on this complex moment,
he writes: "It sums up the whole of New York and its mystical view of deca-

dence. Every special effect can be found here, from sublime verticality to decay on the ground, all the special effects of the mixing of races and empires. This is the fourth dimension of the city."[10] Within a given moment in time, a specific image can present a universe of information, from the "special effect" (a motion picture term) of "sublime verticality to decay on the ground" to the " mixing of races and empires." Within a single image, a wealth of information regarding New York is communicated to the viewer.

Baudrillard's discussion of the simulacrum and the hyperreal only serves to show that much of what is portrayed and seen today—as "reality" or the real—has, in fact, taken a technological turn in its presentation to portray and present a "more than real" image of the real. This phenomenon can equally be seen in advertising; appearances are made to look shinier, more luminous, brighter, faster, and, in general, "better" than they are. For example, over the past decade, New York City's Times Square has displayed a continuing shift into the realm of the hyperreal. There are more lights and more billboards with electronic messages flashing at rapid speed; the area is cleaned and polished, and with its billboards and shops, the area now resembles some sort of Disney World. The shift to presenting and showing the real in a hyperreal manner has become a part of our everyday language; images are accepted, but hyperreal ones are preferred.

In a world in which images have become hyperreal, language has not re-mained unaltered. Words too have taken on a different form. In *Radical Artifice* (1991),[11] Marjorie Perloff examines contemporary poetics and poetry with re-spect to some of the radical changes that have occurred with technology. Con-necting the title of the book with its subtitle, *Writing Poetry in the Age of Media*, Perloff explores and locates contemporary poetry under the influence of tech-nology and the media. Poetry, as Perloff shows, is no longer limited to pen (or pencil) and paper, but in fact, within the new paradigm, it can be found in some of the most immediate, unexpected, and artificial places. These could include highway billboards, digital messages displayed and programmed by computers, advertising leaflets, graphic designs, or even motel signs along the road. Ulti-mately, much of such composed and designed everyday "texts" can be seen and read as poetry.

Today, what is considered a "text" can exist in a variety, or a combination, of different forms: verbal, visual, musical, and others. In 1968, a movement started by predominantly French intellectuals and thinkers, commonly referred to as "poststructuralism," brought about several important reformulations in literary theory, literary and cultural studies, and philosophy.[12] Among these re-formulations are the liberation of "texts" and "language" from the constraints of the author and authorship, and the re-visioning and widening of the definition of text (written and spoken) to include other forms of representation, such as painting or music, as "texts" in and of themselves. Whereas once the notes to Beethoven's Fifth Symphony were seen as purely as notes of musical composition, now the composition could be seen as a "text," and one that could be "read." The same understanding of "texts" applies to other fields such as the fine arts, such as dance, film, and theater.

Extending the understanding of "text" and language to other fields opened an entirely new universe of criticism, expression, and interpretation. As for the theater and the cinema, this redefinition very quickly expanded the possibilities in both art forms—both of which contain multilayered texts (image, sound, music, written word, spoken word, and so on).

With substantial improvements in technology and with the new definition of "text"—in which each single element of a play or a screenplay can be seen as a text of its own—film and theater directors gained a much higher degree of liberty. In the cinema, the "French New Wave" emerged, including figures such as Jean-Luc Godard and François Truffaut, and established the *auteur theory*. A significant contribution of the *auteur* theory to the cinema was the combination of the writer/author and the director into one person. Whereas previously, one or more persons were the "writer" and another person was the director, now, under the *auteur* theory, the director was also the screenwriter. In the "new wave," directors wrote and directed their own films. With this carte blanche also came the liberty of exploring and experimenting with technique and form, as seen, for example, in the numerous jump cuts in Godard's *Breathless* (1960), or the long takes in Truffaut's *400 Blows* (1959).[13]

The influence and impact of the cinema on theater in the United States can be seen shortly thereafter. By the early 1970s, several theater directors had emerged as contemporary *auteur* directors who wrote their own scripts, and employed new technologies to develop and direct their stagings. Of this small group of *auteur* directors, two figures particularly stand out: Robert Wilson and Richard Foreman.

In *The Theatre of Images* (1977), Bonnie Marranca examines three *auteur*-directors of the American theater of the 1970s: Richard Foreman (Ontological-Hysteric Theater), Robert Wilson (Byrd Hoffman School of Byrds) and Lee Breuer (Mabou Mines). Observing the immediacy of images in their work, she describes their theater as a "Theater of Images." With the redefinition of "text" to encompass more than merely the written and spoken word, an important shift occurs on their stage. "Value came increasingly to be placed on performance with the result that the new theatre never became a literary theatre, but one dominated by images—visual and aural."[14]

In addition, the two *auteur*-directors being considered here—Wilson and Foreman—are responsible for their "text"; they are either writing their own original material, or adapting a prewritten work. As a result, such freedom is extended to their stagings as well, in which the stage-image becomes highly formalized and fragmented with a nonconventional plot, character, setting, language, or "realistic" movement. Marranca notes, "Actors do not create 'roles.'

They function instead as media through which the playwright [*auteur*-director] expresses his ideas; they serve as icons and images."[15]

Language continues to exist on par with their stage-images and elements, though with a lesser degree of emphasis. With the diminishing role of language, the importance of the stage-image increases and takes a dominant role. "If this theatre refused to believe in the supremacy of language as a critique of reality, it offered a multiplicity of images in its place."[16]

Different in their approaches, both Wilson and Foreman use their theatrical elements not only to create stage-images, but also to shape the audiences' perceptions of the work. In the case of Wilson, this impact is often achieved through a highly structured, slow motion choreography, along with often repetitive and minimalist music. Foreman uses text softly spoken over microphones along with special sound effects to attain this emotional impact in his audience. At other times, the opposite may hold true. For example, in *Now That Communism Is Dead, I Feel My Life Is Over* (2001), the audience was randomly exposed to loud sound effects, and sound became an integral component of the stage-image.

In creating their stage-images, both Wilson and Foreman also allow themselves to play with and (re)define stage-time. They expand or contract it depending on the effect they wish to have upon the audience. In this sense, with time distortion at work, their theater becomes "timeless";[17] the images can be framed in such a way as to be either fast or slow to the point of being "static." As for the space to contain their images, both directors also design their own sets. A distinguishing signature of their design, which they hold in common, is that their stage almost always allows an image to be framed—as in a two-dimensional tableau. In his production *White Raven* (2001), a collaboration with Philip Glass, Wilson portrayed a stormy ocean with various layers of flat waves, covering the span of the stage, while moving vertically up and down to the music. Foreman, on the other hand, achieves this two-dimensional stage effect through a tightness of scenery along with a compressed space and the use of many props. With respect to his most recent stagings, Foreman refers to his work as "dense";[18] the stage space becomes an arena in which everything—text, sound, music, prop, set, and other stage elements—is compressed into a single frame. Despite their different backgrounds and individual approaches, both Wilson and Foreman have greatly enriched the art of creating images on stage.

The shift from spoken/written language to imagery in the theater of Wilson and Foreman parallels the poststructuralists' shift from spoken/written language to language within a broader context and understood in different modes. Before this intersection, within the American theater, such a shift from word to image had not been fully explored to the extent that Wilson and Foreman have undertaken. The theater had produced *auteur*-directors (for example, Richard Schechner and André Gregory in the 1960s), but none with such a high degree of audiovisual sophistication in their stage vocabulary. This shift can well be seen as a rupture in the history and tradition of the theater. As Marranca points out, "This break from a theatrical structure founded on dialogue marks a watershed in the history of American theater, a *rite of passage*."[19] In examining the works of two *auteur*-directors, we find that they greatly differ in philosophy and practice. Both employ comparable approaches to their source texts, but their end results are quite different.

Robert Wilson: Painter in Time

In Robert Wilson's stage, the images are often provided by human figures that are sharply defined by posture, costume, and light, all moving in a distinct manner to a given rhythm. More often than not, the movements are slow, minimal, and repetitive; they require multiple hours of rehearsal to achieve the required perfection of the image. Wilson's stage-images are primarily derived from everyday movements and gestures, as well as from memories from his personal history. The selected actors (in rehearsals, they are often referred to by numbers instead of by names) are professionals as well as nonprofessionals who have a predisposition for visual memory and a keen sense of movement. On his stage, along with his well-sculpted and precisely choreographed moving figures, there is a set almost always designed by Wilson himself.

Having been trained as a designer, Wilson draws on clearly defined structures, shapes, and forms to create his stage-images and set design. In addition to this visual training, Wilson also worked extensively with dance and movement, specifically with respect to assisting the physically handicapped.[20] In 1968, Wilson moved to a loft in downtown Manhattan, which he used as both a place of residence and a performance space. The loft was soon named "The Byrd Hoffman School of Byrds," a location for performances and a variety of projects. The "school" included Wilson and his circle of friends, supporters, and collaborators.[21] Staging productions with the handicapped still remained a large part of Wilson's work with the school. Not unlike Foreman's use of stage-images to provoke a reaction in his audience, Wilson used his work to enable a group to interact with one another and, in some cases, to react and respond to images. Robyn Brentano, an original member of the Byrd School, recalls an early experience with such a performance:

> I remember Bob did a theatre piece with the patients on C-12, which was a ward of polio victims who were either in iron lungs or on respirators. A lot of them used mouth sticks to draw or write or turn the pages of a book and Bob tied strings between the various people in the unit. He darkened the room and brought in a black light so the strings glowed. I think it was a very moving experience for those people because it allowed them to be in contact with each other in a way other than yelling across the room. Many of the patients were

completely paralyzed so the work he was doing was extremely minimal, often more mental than physical. He just basically got them to work with what they were hearing and what they were thinking and the very, very small movements they were able to make. One of the interesting things about Bob was that he was able to reach people who were terminal in their attitudes or in some way numbed by living within an institutional setting, in some cases for decades. He could get patients to respond by bringing them to the window to look at boats on the river or listen to steam in the pipes or watch the plants growing in the solarium. The whole point of his work was that he tried to get people to open up and be much more aware of the small things in their environment.[22]

It was also during these Byrd Hoffman days when his long collaboration with Christopher Knowles, an autistic boy of fourteen, began. Knowles and Wilson developed a very close relationship, which resulted in many productions, the primary ones being *A Letter for Queen Victoria* (1974), *The $ Value of Man* (1975), and the *Dia logs* (1975). Wilson credits Knowles for a great deal of inspiration and material he contributed: "I was fascinated from the very beginning with what Chris was doing with language. He'd take words we all know and fracture them and then put them back together in a new way. He'd invent a new language and then destroy it a moment later. Words are like molecules that are always changing their configurations, breaking apart and recombining. It's very free and alive. Language is his own kingdom."[23] The collaboration with Christopher Knowles, as Wilson points out, was already alluding to and indicating Wilson's future use of language and text in his theater. The prologue for *A Letter for Queen Victoria*, for example, included images with sound, movement, and a highly fragmented text in the form of a duet between Bob Wilson and Christopher Knowles.

Through such collaborations during his early days as a theater director, Wilson also developed his sensibility for time, slow motion, and an affinity for textual ruptures—all particular elements that form the basis for his stage aesthetics. Shortly after the *Queen Victoria* production, Wilson moved away from the Byrd School, towards formulating his aesthetics as an *auteur*-director of the theater.

His directorial approach places emphasis on "stage visions" as texts. He therefore transforms all his source texts—whether they are his own work, the product of collaboration with other artists, or classical texts—into his own unique stage-images. As with Foreman, if not more so, Wilson's approach to the written text remains the same in each case. For him, the text serves as a proto-text, or a "pretext" to create his preformulated stagings: a world of images, of a multiplicity of references, and of time-elapsed slow motions. Very little (if any) text is used in his original pieces, and when using existing texts, whether by Shakespeare or Heiner Müller, Wilson takes the liberty of rearranging, displacing, and redistributing them so as to create a nonnarrative structure that juxtaposes itself to the other layers of his stagings. For him, words become sounds, sounds become images,[24] and the original text remains only as a "trace" that will be reconstructed by the spectator. His images and designs remain at the center of his stagings. The final result, offered to the viewer, is one in which the many threads are woven together into a complex, multilayered spectacle. In this regard, Wilson's work, as we shall see, shares a common denominator with Foreman's original pieces. The final product presented to the audience is one in which the threads of dissemination combine to create a multilayered event. Sound, text, and images exist on equal footing with one another, and the original text, be it Shakespeare's *Hamlet* or Müller's *Hamletmachine*, becomes a trace that the audience has to realign with the other elements to arrive at an interpretation, if they care to do so.

Wilson's sets contain elements from everyday life as well as from world history. Objects range from ancient Greek icons and Egyptian hieroglyphs to television screens and airplanes. The set is predominantly composed and designed in conjunction with the lighting, and usually, the light itself becomes part of the scenes, acting as a constituting event.[25] One spectacular moment of such use of light can be seen in *Einstein on the Beach* (1976). Wilson had a horizontal bar of light move very slowly across the stage to the music of Philip Glass. The moment ended with the bar arriving at center stage and then slowly rotating to a vertical position. The moment was captivating to watch as it was implemented with a tremendous amount of mastery and precision, while the light itself radiated, illuminated the stage, and created both an aura and a drama of its own. The technique has been used since, and one can find it in stagings as recent as Wilson's collaboration with Philip Glass, *White Raven* (2001). Here, he once again makes use of light as an active part of the set and scene: In this production, he had a circle of blue light slowly travel horizontally across the stage.

Wilson likes to label his stagings as "operas," even though some of them do not have music. Among the composers who have collaborated with Wilson, are Tom Waits, David Byrne of the music band The Talking Heads, and Philip Glass.[26] Wilson's aesthetics, therefore, are a combination of layered elements of different artwork. Each element exists independent of the other, and yet in total unity; his "operas" (or staged works) mirror Brecht and Weill's notion of opera.[27]

In staging Ibsen's *When We Dead Awaken* at the American Repertory Theater (1991),[28] Wilson's approach to the play was similar to the approach he takes with his own text. The final product did not differ much aesthetically from previous productions because the Ibsen text, adapted by Robert Brustein, once again served as a proto-text for Wilson's stage-images. In staging the text, Wilson divided his rehearsals into different phases: Phase A, B, and C, each having a different directing element involved.

Wilson started off by drawing charcoal sketches of images he saw for the play. Each drawing was done precisely not only to reflect one moment that he envisioned, but also done to reflect a specific perspective of light—some extremely dark, others rather light. Based on these drawings, Wilson designed the stage, the props, and the furniture.

For his auditions, Wilson would perform a simple task of walking and then sitting, and he would then ask the actors to imitate his motions as accurately as possible while he watched. The ones who could replicate his motions most accurately, and therefore had a good visual memory, were selected for the production. As for the production process itself, Wilson referred to the actors using numbers.[29] Using a limited movement vocabulary—with each movement having a letter and a number: C15, K7, etc.—he would then give certain movements to the different actors at different times, announcing the movement number over a microphone. Additionally, all rehearsals were also videotaped.

In this manner, independent of Ibsen's text, or Brustein's adaptation, Wilson created his stage world—"a theater of vision"—and then proceeded to complete it by inserting the text in retrospect. Interspersed within the production were also Wilson's "entr'actes"—a device he had used in the past with respect to his self-generated texts. The entr'actes, in this case, were brief and "humorous" moments, which he called the "knee plays."[30]

Such, then, was the process of rendering Ibsen's text for the stage. And such has been Wilson's *auteur*-director approach to the theater. For some audience members, the results of his stagings, particularly in his *self-generated texts* versus the *prewritten* texts, work well; for others, they do not because they feel they are seeing yet another Wilson text overriding a play by Ibsen or Shakespeare.

For Müller, who collaborated on a number of projects with Wilson, the work resulted in a very satisfactory final product. The two men came from opposite ends of the world:

> Nothing illustrates the gulf between their respective experiences of the world more vividly than the earliest childhood memories of each man. Müller's first recollection is of Nazi brownshirts coming in the night to arrest his father, a Socialist Democrat, hours after Hitler had taken power, while Wilson remembers the layout of the neighborhood supermarket with its neatly arranged produce section, gleaming linoleum aisles and checkout counters (though as Müller points out this model of order and regularity was not without its own terrors).[31]

Yet, this kind of opposition has yielded many successful collaborations.

Though Müller's texts are heavily historical, political, and culturally specific, Wilson directs them regardless of their content, most times not even interpreting them. Against interpretation, Wilson sees the texts as sounds and music, sources for his proto-text. Wilson works against the preexisting text to create a presentation composed of finely mixed elements, a kind of *soufflé du théâtre*. In a three-and-a-half hour staging of Müller's *Hamletmachine* with New York University undergraduates (1986), Wilson did not replicate even one of the images prescribed in the text: Not a single phrase or stage direction was illustrated. For Müller, this was not only a valid approach, but one that he recommended to other directors: Müller was interested in conflicts and "civil wars," and he saw clashes as a source of artistic productivity.[32]

In a 1991 interview, Müller remarked that he saw conflicts as a form of communication as well as a source of creativity.[33] With regard to Wilson, Müller stated that their collaboration was one of clashes, conflicts, and "civil war," and that made it valid: "Bob drinks Vodka, I drink Scotch. That's a civil war." This "civil war" is what Müller likes in Wilson's stagings: Wilson's texts remain autonomous of Müller, and are deeply layered without getting meshed. If anything, Wilson manages to remain faithful to Müller's *synthetic fragments*[34] by creating more ruptures, more fragmentation, and more layers of meaning, thus being faithful by being unfaithful to the text "in a postmodern manner." Müller welcomed Wilson's stagings of his texts, pointing out that nothing is lost: "Bob treats a text like a piece of furniture. He doesn't try to break it up or break it open or try to get information out of it or meaning or emotion. It's just a thing. That's what I like about his way because a text can stand for itself. It doesn't need support, it doesn't need help."[35] Elsewhere, Müller refers to his texts as "stones lying at the bottom of a river, submerged in Wilson's imagery which flows around them without discoloring or obscuring them." Using the same metaphor, Wilson talks about Müller's texts as "rocks which can be put in the snow, in the sand, in the ocean or in outer space and their state is not altered."[36] Müller comments:

> I have no message, I just want conflicts, even between the audience and the text. . . . I am now fifty-six or something and for the last forty years all they have talked about in Germany is this year's concepts. It's so boring. I have them, it's no problem. There is no reason to talk about them. In the fifties I watched rehearsals at the Berliner Ensemble. When an actor got an idea—'You know I think it should be, etc.'—Brecht would say, 'Show it, don't discuss it, show it.' There were no discussions. That's why I like working with Bob. He has a visual concept and it's compelling. He gives you something and you can deal with that and you don't have to talk concepts or ideas. It's stupid. It's theatre and theatre is not ideas. You shouldn't have to remember your ideas like in school, you just get the image and maybe in the next four weeks you work with the ideas you get from it in that moment.[37]

Müller points out that interpretation is the audience's job, and it shouldn't happen on stage. As for Wilson, Müller reinforces the fact that "text is merely pretext—a scenario."[38] He remarks that: "Bob leaves the text alone. He never tries to be interpretive."[39]

For both Wilson and Foreman—and much of late twentieth-century theater which pursued similar ideas—the theater becomes a space for artistic creation and its presentation, using the text as one theatrical element among the many. Stage-images are presented to the audience in their full richness—with all the different elements at work—and the audience is invited to watch, and walk away with an archive of images stored in their "museum of memories,"[40] enabling the images to resonate and produce meaning with time. Yet, despite the usage of fragmented text and the heavy emphasis on visual elements, Wilson's stage-images are not cinematic images. Cinematic images must be real, or give the illusion of reality. Wilson's images defy this characteristic, since they are often in slow motion and are stylized.

Richard Foreman: Sculpting with Sound

Richard Foreman is equally well-known and regarded as one of the most influential figures of the late twentieth-century avant-garde theater. A winner of numerous awards, Foreman largely "invents" (his word choice over "creates") his stage-images from textual fragments, sound, and spatial configurations, and presents the results to his audience as a highly self-contained "reality."[41] For Foreman, the stage reality—what is presented and seen on stage—no matter how stylized, simple, or complex it may be, *is* what defines the *real*.

To make his vision of the stage-image "real"—not to be confused with "realistic"—Foreman uses every possible device to create distancing. This is quite related to Brecht's *verfremdungseffekt*, often abbreviated the "V-effect," which refers to the use of a device to distance the observers from the observed to enable them to assume a critical stance toward the performance.[42] In Foreman's case, the "V-effect" is accomplished in a variety of ways. His actors are almost always microphoned, and the audience can only hear them through speakers, much like in the cinema. Movements and language, along with the many layers of sound, noise, and music, are all stylized; Foreman is presenting his vision of "reality," but there is nothing in his work or on his stage that pretends to be realistic, or a copy of the outside world. The material (the "text" in its broadest sense, including all theatrical elements) is simply presented, and the audience, flooded by a wealth of information in different forms, is invited to construe and put together, as in a jigsaw puzzle, the reality that they have encountered on the stage.

The presentation of the material often takes on different forms. As Foreman once described it during an interview in 2001, "I have thought in the past that, it is as if my texts are the patient, and in staging them I'm the analyst." With such an approach, and with Foreman's highly evolved stage technology, the invented (or construed) reality can take many shapes. It can span anywhere from a softly spoken, slow motion dialogue between two people to a hyperactive contemporary circus in which life, politics, and social, psychological, and philosophical issues are being represented in a multitude of forms.

Foreman, like Wilson, places his emphasis not only on visual images as part of his stage-images, but also on other components that can contribute to and become a part of the stage-image, though the visual elements usually take precedence. Aware of his strong visual abilities and inclination, he explains how he works with the text and the stage, drawing a contrast with Robert Wilson:

> I'm visually very sophisticated, but I don't think in terms of making images. I wish I could get rid of scenery. I mean, to me, the most interesting experience I have of my plays is when I first sort of put them together and I'm sitting here and I'm reading very casually . . . again, what is this play about this year: "ah it's a racing car . . . oh yes, this is a scene with pancakes." And all that just vaguely flutters through my mind against a background, not focused on it, this wall which has no reality, it's all in limbo, and I would like to get that limbo sense in the theater. I think I do to a certain extent and the complexity of the décor creates that because it's sort of unreadable. It's so busy, it's sort of like a blur in the background; but I hate scenery. I also hate my sense of color. I wish I could think of a new color that would be a non-color. So, obviously these visual issues are important to me in a way, but they are not important in the sense that Bob Wilson is visual in that he's trying to make striking pictures. I'm really not interested in that. I'm only interested in a kind of psycho-spiritual tension. I can see that images resolve; often times there are images, but that's not something I worry about. They're on stage, it's a moment which combines sound, light, gesture, together they make something balanced on the edge of life, an attempt to evade all categories.[43]

Referring to his stage-images as "something balanced on the edge of life," while at the same time trying "to evade categories" and labels, Foreman describes his theater as a "hovercraft theater," where "everything is vibrating, everything is whirling around, everything is hovering in space."[44] This "hovering" description holds particularly true on Foreman's stage, as the different elements are almost always in a constant state of either being stylized, or distanced, or both.

The stylization and distancing—a theatrical technique dating back to Bertolt Brecht—serves a specific purpose. It enables the audience to observe the highly dense reality presented on stage, rather than being pulled into it and potentially identifying with it. Not only is Foreman's use of distancing not far from what Brecht wanted to obtain with his theater, but it is, in many ways, a contemporary form of it. Foreman often and openly cites Brecht as one of the primary influences in his theater work:

> Very early on I knew I was revolting, which is why when I was fifteen or so I discovered first references to Brecht, and they talked about Brecht being clinical, not asking for empathy. Ah! That was meaning to open the flood gate, and that was something I could relate to as opposed to the American theater at the time. This was very early 50s.[45]

In inventing a "reality" for his stage, Foreman wants the stage to present and represent, and the audience to be intellectually awake and attentive to the multidimensional reality of what is being presented. In unity with Brecht, Foreman acknowledges his dislike for popular theater, which is performance-centric and demands emotional responses from the audience. He describes his affinity for "theater that did not particularly appeal on the emotional level, but tried to have a certain clinical coldness so that the spectator could sit back detached and observe what he was seeing. For me that was like the opening of a window. Because even at the age of fifteen, I used to go see all the Broadway shows and feel that they were sentimental, that they were pandering to the audience and trying to manipulate the audience. I had no use for practically any of the shows that were hits."[46]   Referring to such trends in the theater, from Broadway to Jerzy Grotowski, Foreman emphasizes his dislike for such forms of performance-centric theater where one is "supposed to, in one way or another, love and admire the performer and the performer's virtuosity. Your entry into the world of the play was through the performer, and that's not what I was interested in." What Foreman's stage is interested in obtaining from its audience-stage relationship is precisely the opposite: it wishes to present a reality to a small number of spectators for observation and analysis rather than emotional empathy.

In the past decade, Foreman's work has moved away from text to various technical effects. He describes this shift as one toward creating a stage that has a higher level of density, and even "humanism." Rather than being a detriment—a chaotic distraction of sorts—the complexity and density of the different layers work together to create a stage reality that echoes life. "I am continually interested, in all levels of my work, in generating complicated structures from relatively simple building blocks in ways that I think echo the way life operates."[47]

The stage reality of Foreman is not only an "echo of how life operates," but it is also a mirror of how "the real" functions in life. This multilayered aspect of reality exists in the world on a daily basis. Sounds, visual signs, words, and dialogues can be heard on the street, for example. This experience is present at very early age, when the consciousness begins to process a variety of signals. Remembering his childhood, Foreman recalls an incident with his parents, in which such a multilayered reality was distinctly apparent to him: "I remember when I was a very young boy, riding in the car with my mother, and at one point saying to her, 'You know, even when you're scolding me and I'm scared and unhappy, at the same time I'm singing a little song in my head.' The fact that multiple states of being exist in us at all times is what I'm always trying to express."[48]

Before inventing such a density on stage, the script needs to be open to such a capacity. While a student of playwriting at Yale, Foreman experienced a shift from writing conventional plays to his multilayered texts, partially as a result of being exposed to the underground filmmakers in New York, and partially as a result of being exposed to and "reading the French structuralists and poststructuralists."[49]   As a part of this exposure, his writing developed a nonlinear fragmented style. In line with many of the poststructuralists, Foreman rejects "the realist or authoritarian heresy that the critic (director) can make definitive contact with some ultimate, residual meaning, when, in reality, he is transcribing a code—a series of interlocking codes which can be deciphered but never fully recovered."[50] Foreman points out the impact of poststructuralist thinkers on his work: "And all of these people were so conversant with the possibility of generating literature with less conscious, external control, so I just think that gradually I felt a little more confidence in letting some of my old habits, like writing down character names and stage directions, fall away. I felt freer to just say, 'Well, I'm generating these texts which I, as the director, will figure out how to stage somehow, even though these texts really aren't plays at all.'"[51]

With his "nonplays," the productions became more layered by way of texts, props, sounds, and other stage elements. In addition to his "non-play" multilayered scripts, Foreman also chose to move into a much smaller space. As a result of this shift, objects, movements, and other stage elements have been forced to become more compact. Once again, not seen as a disadvantage, but as an improvement of the stage-images he wishes to invent, the small space is ultimately privileged over the larger ones. Referring to his theater as a multidimensional one, Foreman remarks:

> I'd like to think of it as eight-dimension theater, really I would . . . String theory; I'd like to think there are dimensions folded up. But it is more multidimensional because it is so small. In other words, I used to have a theater which was very deep, and I think that wasn't as multidimensional, because you were dominated by the depth -- that was one dimension. Everything is like in a compactor, squeezed together.[52]

As a set designer, interested not only in altering the physical space, but also in creating a distance between his stage reality and the audience, for the past four years, Foreman has also added a glass wall between the audience and the stage. This addition to his stage design and space construction is not so much to increase the self-contained nature of the space, but to add yet another level of distancing to his aesthetics:

> The glass wall in front of the actors, that's mostly because I am working in a very small theater where it gives me a certain aesthetic distance which I find desirable. Each year I think I'm not going to use it and then I have to finally since I needed it. There's no question that the décor has become more and more cluttered, and that relates to the density I'm talking about.[53]

In designing the text and the stage-images, the textual transformation not only occurs in the realm of space and visuals, but quite often it also occurs in the realm of sound and sound design. Even though the visual is at the core of his work, Foreman also tries to emphasis the sound, though he finds the process, in relation to the visual elements, to be more challenging than meets the eye. He points out: "I'm trying to fight that, but it's very hard. It's very hard. I'm constantly wishing I could find a way to make the listening be more important, and I find it very difficult to do that."[54] Despite the challenges involved, Foreman has succeeded in bringing in an innovative approach to sound and the sound design, specifically as it pertains to the microphoning of the actors and the use of sound loops. Foreman points out how microphoning creates an additional distancing effect for his stage-image:

> I've been using radio mikes so that the actors don't have to project at all. I don't like their voices when they have to project. I always make sound loops. I have for fifteen years. So, I go into rehearsal with forty, fifty different loops and in rehearsal we try different things, and I change it. Sometimes I have to get more loops, because the ones I chose after three weeks usually don't seem right. But again: it's having all these materials available lying around which I know I am going to mix together—collage together.[55]

For Foreman—a veritable sound designer—using sound on par with visuals may be a challenge, but not one from which he shies away. Loud, unexpected sounds, microphoned text, and the use of "loops"—another level of fragmenting text for the stage reality—all work together to add more layers of text to the "script." Foreman describes the arbitrary manner in which he would select pieces from the radio to form loops for his productions:

> I'd turn the radio to certain stations I liked and hear things, and then I'd run over and try to push the tape recorder in time to catch what I thought was interesting in that it had a potential loop on it. Then I would take that tape and find a little section, three seconds or so that I liked, which I would make a loop out of, and then I would record that loop onto a cassette so that it ran for half an hour. And I would write to that . . . well, to two of them playing simultaneously.[56]

The added loops, which are often not synchronized, not only give another layer of text to the stage-image, but they also increase the nonlinear density on stage. Foreman comments on this aspect of the loops:

> What's interesting to me is the way that two loops, obviously not having exactly the same rhythm, obviously not being exactly the same length—it means that you are generating a world of continual change using the simplest elements, you see. Because the loops come into synch perhaps, what, every five minutes let's say, and otherwise their relationship to each other will always be shifting, so that you are creating a continually changing structure using the simple elements of this two- or three-second repeating loop.[57]

In contrast to his complicated, busy, complex multileveled and multilayered stage, Foreman's stage-images can sometimes be extremely still—creating a two-dimensional stage effect. However, as with the sound effects, the still images also contain spurts of dynamic movement interspersed throughout the staging. To attain this stillness in his stage-images, Foreman refers to having his actors stand still quite a bit of the time and move very rarely, and slowly, for the most part. Once again, with this alienation effect in the stage movement, the audience is able to focus within the frame and into the tableaux. Foreman explains:

> Yes, they [the actors] spent a lot of the evening standing in tableaux. It would hold for five or six lines, and then there'd be a slight shift, and hold for another five or six lines. Another slight shift, five or six lines. And then a ludicrous, exaggerated action, like tumbling through the window. And as one tumbled through the window, then holding an awkward position at the end of that tumble for five or six lines."[58]

Here again, it becomes apparent that the text is not the dominant aspect of Foreman's stage-image, but rather just a part of it—just as much as movement, sound, and lights are. With such a degree of control over the various stage elements, Foreman manages to create a stage-image that, much like a two-dimensional framed image, is "static." The production becomes, as he refers to it, a "continual static tableau, followed by slight adjustment, followed by occasional, rather spectacular, but awkward activity."[59]

Richard Foreman's influence on the contemporary theater can be found in other recognized theater artists and theater companies. A prime example is Elizabeth Le Compte's Wooster Group. The Wooster Group, a direct descendant of the Performing Garage started by Richard Schechner in the 1960s, in many ways parallels Foreman's group, with whom they have collaborated several times. In recalling one piece they did together, *Miss Universal Happiness* (1985), Richard Foreman explains the intensity of loud music, movement, and dynamic involved:

> In the staging of the piece I could indulge in asking for more violent physical activity. We built a set that had ramps leading up to walls, and people would run up the ramps and smack against these very solid walls. But generally, because they were used to a similar kind of work, in a technical way, there was no problem for them to adjust to my extremely choreographed direction. And since they threw themselves into it with a vengeance, the piece could get very fast. I remember once or twice when I started explaining motivations they would say, Oh come on, Richard, that's what you tell regular actors; you don't have to give us motivations, just tell us what to do. Of course, not every moment was loud, but there were a lot of explosions of activity and violence.[60]

In working on sound and music for *Miss Universal Happiness* with the Wooster Group, Foreman points out, "Since the Wooster Group people in one way or another were more into rock 'n' roll than my actors normally are, I think that also pushed them in that direction, because those song forms got very energetic and were delivered almost like big rap or rock numbers." With this fast paced production, Foreman came to use the handheld microphones for the first time: "It was also the first time that I used a lot of stand or handheld microphones, and that contributed to the high energy of the piece. Those songs were very important in the piece. And it may be that *Miss Universal Happiness* was the first play in which certain sections were written to the tape loops."

In another collaboration with the Wooster Group, Foreman only used four actors, so that "the work could be more intimate." Here, rather than having a physical approach, as he tended to do, he wanted "to pull them towards a more naturalistic, more psychological kind of performance than they had given, either in my previous work or in the work that they normally do for the Wooster Group. And I think they did. I was working a lot on trying to make them do a subdued, more internalized kind of performance."[61] The opposite of the fast, loud, chaotic stagings of texts, this quiet, more internalized performance was a style that was to become part of Foreman's vocabulary. This softening of delivery and internalization of the text made it appear as if the actor was "mulling over what he was going to do with himself. You see the performer making decisions vis-à-vis his own consciousness."[62] The product—a shift from the fast-paced, loud, rock 'n' roll tempo, to a more psychological, hypnotic-like stage where the audience would then be seeing the actor struggle with his or her thoughts—would allow the audience to think that "he's intellectually struggling with ideas, or with trying to have an effect upon his own psyche." Foreman sees this step as a new addition to his stage work: "And that's the shift in my work: Now the performer is no longer someone who presents something to the audience, but rather is somebody privately working on himself, fully consciousness of what he is doing."[63]

Comparing the avant-garde approach used by himself and Le Compte with a traditional mode of theater, Foreman notes that the need for a multiplicity of events is what distinguishes both Le Compte and himself from any "other theater." In an interview with Le Compte, Foreman elaborates: "That defines the real anti-theatrical tradition, which you and I are into, as opposed to that other Ibsenite tradition that still demands you craft the audience's attention towards that specific 'important' thing that is supposed to happen inside your preconceived premise. And once you've thrown out that notion, you're in a new theatrical world."[64]

To this day, the Wooster Group has maintained many aesthetic elements that are similar to Foreman's work and style, such as the multiplicity of events happening on the stage at the same time and the handheld microphones. However, they have also developed their own aesthetics and use of technology, for example, the successful incorporation of video into their productions by way of video monitors and television screens.

In many ways, Foreman's aesthetics and directorial practice, which seeks to create a multilayered, dense reality, share many common denominators with the cinema. Writing in a fragmented and montaged manner, creating distancing by microphoning the actors, and placing a glass wall between the audience and the

stage are key examples of this. However, despite all these transformations and
innovations Foreman still refers to his work simply as "art" or as "theater."[65]

The influence of cinema on Foreman's aesthetics goes back to his last years
as a graduate student at Yale School of Drama, when he first encountered underground filmmaking and Jonas Mekas, one of its *auteurs*. "It was like nothing
I'd ever seen. I remember being very moved by Ron Rice and his use of music,
and other things in the film. After that first night I started going back, and pretty
soon I was spending all my time, many nights a week, going to see these
screenings, because a lot of material started to come out at that point. And that
changed, radically, how I saw everything."[66] For Foreman the playwriting student, the world of playwriting was transformed through interactions with cinema.

The influence of cinema on Foreman can be seen in many elements of his
work: from the generation of a script through montage, to the final, polished
stage-image. In describing his approach to writing his own scripts, he explains
that he does not write in a linear and structured manner, but rather with a strictly
nonlinear sequence and narrative. Additionally, much like the montage process
in the cinema, the moments are generated one at a time and are only compiled
into a script at the end:

> I write—usually at the beginning of the day, from one-half to three pages of
> dialogue. There is no indication who is speaking—just raw dialogue. From day
> to day, there is no connection between the pages, each day is a total 'start from
> scratch' with no necessary reference to material from previous day's work.
> (Though it sometimes—infrequently—happens that there is a thematic carryo-
> ver).[67]

In recent years, Foreman has begun to write and rewrite his scripts, rather
than writing through a nonlinear montage process. The approach of creating a
multilayered stage very much parallels cinema's montage theory. Yet, despite
their many similarities, the stage-image in the theater of Richard Foreman dif-
fers in many ways from the cinema and its cinematic image.

For Foreman, who has made one feature film, the theater still remains closer
to him as an artist as well as to reality. For an *auteur* who enjoys inventing and
representing his own perspective of reality on the stage, cinema and the cinematic image can be too realistic. Rather than showing *the real*, the cinema
shows an *illusion of the real*. "Film, especially since almost all films are now
shot on location, whatever the adventure is that is going on, film convinces you
that it takes place in the real world."[68] The photographic element in the film-
image by its very allusion to the real, can not only dictate what is real, but also
what is, or might be, better:

> It's not only that what can't be photographed can't be real, but what photo-
> graphs better is more important and more real. In other words, if Elizabeth

Taylor photographs better than some kind of electron pattern with an electron microscope, that proves that she is more important. And if Elizabeth Taylor photographs better than Mary Jane, who sells newspapers on the corner, that proves Elizabeth Taylor is somehow more important than Mary Jane.[69]

Foreman likens this photographic nature of the film image, which can allure the audience to such a high degree, as you find in "the Judeo-Christian religion [when it] says: Don't worship graven images." Understanding the impact of films and the visual arts on audience and contemporary culture, Foreman remarks: "Basically we live in a visually oriented culture, and images tend to become icons that we assimilate without really relating to, without weaving them into the warp and woof of our everyday reality. And it sort of makes one believe that the real world that is perceived is the only possible world."[70]

For Foreman, the cinema-image is only an illusion of the real, not a copy or a truthful representation of the real. It captures an image of the present and shows it in the future, and in doing so, the presented image maintains its presence—the false sign of being in the present—while, in reality, it existed in the past. The theater, on the other hand, is real in its presence: objects, people, and actors are there in the present moment, even if they are spatially distanced. In cinema, there is only a captured image of what was in the past, and in addition to a spatial distancing, there is a temporal distancing. Foreman's main objection to the cinema lies in this temporal distancing. For Foreman the theater *auteur*, "real" is only real when it is in the present before you:

That sense of distancing [in the cinema] does not operate for me. I think if I see something on film, it was really was there; it's proof that it really was there. In the theater, obviously, the scenery is not a real brick wall, it's obviously alluding to a brick wall. And the way you perform in front of the audience, the way the actors are moving are, in my sense, making allusions to real life, because it's never real life. It is a ceremony in a room in front of other people. And there is no other situation in the world like that; it's artificial, so you can exploit that artificiality.[71]

In Foreman's philosophy of theater, it is the real that needs to be staged and shown, and this is none other than the experiences and understanding of the writer-director. Imagination, multilayered texts, and scenery, sound, and other aesthetic devices can be at work to create this reality. However, as a result of their being rooted in the present before the audience, they will remain real, as opposed to the screen, which by its cinematic image will create an illusion of the real because it is relocating the past into the present. Comparing the imagination working in both domains to invent "another world, another time, another reality,"[72] Foreman remarks:

Even with Fellini, you are filming real people who are acting grotesquely. You cannot suggest that intuition on another level of reality. Now I would say, today that's not true. I wouldn't say Fellini does it particularly, but of course I grew up in New York, [and] a seminal influence for me when I got out of college was encountering the underground film movement in New York City, however very abstract filmmakers. I knew, even though I made one feature film, that I was not a filmmaker. Somehow I just have the theater in my blood and I feel confident and I know how to do things in the theater. In film, I just don't have that feeling, even though I see many, many films. But I do think that there is a problem with film in trying to escape the giving up of physical life on earth. I want to escape that, and I think in theater there are ways that do slightly suggest the other realm exists. You don't have to film it, you don't have to take pictures of it, you know, which then turns them into another 3-D photographical art of reality. You can allude to them in other ways. Now people can argue of course that in film and in cinema, that somehow, because it is film, you see that what you are seeing, film, is part of the same material as that material in your apartment or on the street, and so on.[73]

As an "inventor of realities," for Foreman, what matters is not the *real* in the *realistic* sense of the word, but rather the real as that which has an actual presence, in the temporal sense of the word, in the here and now of the space: with the stage and its audience. With this definition in mind, in the theater of Foreman, any "invented reality" is *real*.

For his next production, Foreman is using fifty sentences, with three lead actresses and five actors—a total of eight—to create a full production. The secret for this production, this reality, lies in the fact that the fifty lines of text are to be prerecorded by Foreman, using his own voice, in different pitches and modules. As he has pointed out, the line between his text/stage and production/stage-images is not well defined; they are one and the same, but in different forms. "Well, the plays are all about me and my trying to stage my particular rhythms and perceptions, so it's only fair. . . . Someday maybe I'll be in the play myself. Maybe not, but my voice has always been present in the play. And now technology allows a way for me to put my face in the play sometimes too, when I think it's appropriate."[74] For this production, Foreman has already built a model, but he is quick to point out that "all will change."[75]

As an innovator and well-recognized figure of the American avant-garde theater in the late twentieth century, Foreman has not only been a great influence on other theater directors and companies, but he also continues to push his artistic and creative limits. Despite his sometimes "static" stage-images, he is not static; he is constantly evolving, developing, and producing, though, he still wants to explore more, discover more, and reach new results:

Sometimes I feel, no, I always feel I'm not radical enough, I'm not going far enough. I imagine things that are much more radical than I am able to do, and then I start rehearsing. A lot of my ideas about things are very radical things but end up seeming obvious and stupid, and my plays end up by coming back closer to what I normally do. So, I do think I take little tiny steps forward each time. They are not the giant steps I dream about, but the giant steps I dream about, then, don't seem true to some inner necessity I guess I experience.[76]

Undoubtedly, inventing realities or images for either the screen or the theater is not a simple task; it will take thought, effort, and careful definitions. If in the theater of Robert Wilson and Richard Foreman an element is lacking to bring it close to the aesthetics and form of the cinema, it is precisely that which they have actively been shunning and/or redefining: the real and realism. If Foreman defines the "real" as that which is temporally located in the present, but uses prerecorded sounds as an element of distancing, his theater could be argued as *not* "real." On the other hand, if the real is seen as an entity in relation to time—past, present, and future—then an image captured in the past shows what was "real." Such, for example, is the nature of documentary films. By viewing a documentary on nature or World War II, we cannot argue whether it was real or not; whether it existed or not, and whether such reality occurred or not. Real can be: It can be in the past, it can be in the present, and it can be in the future.

Film captures images from the present for the future. In a sense, it can be called a "timeless" form of art, even more so than the theater, as the theater only exists in the present, whereas films spans all three levels of time. Additionally, if film can tell a "lie" and create a (photographic) "illusion," the same can be said of theater: It too can tell a lie by attempting to create a "reality" on stage that, as "real" as it may be, remains an "illusion." This occurs due to the simple fact that it *is* theater, and the curtain falls and the audience claps at the end of the performance, applauding the "reality" they just witnessed. This mechanism equally holds true for the stylized stage and stage-images of Robert Wilson and Richard Foreman, as it does for the most "realistic" plays on Broadway.

Although in creating their stage-images, neither Wilson nor Foreman are attempting to create cinematic images, among the current theater *auteurs*, their work comes closest to the cinematic theater and its stage. Where both Wilson and Foreman fail to create a cinematic theater is in their definition, or lack thereof, of the "real," along with an overemphasis on fragmentation and multi-layeredness of the stage, which allows no room for structural narrative unity, and no possibility of "realism." In the cinematic theater, the theatrical elements come together to create a unified aesthetic whole, whereby both the theater space, the stage, can exist along with the play or screenplay—*A Streetcar Named Desire*, for example—without being forced into fragmentation or showing disdain for the "real" and "realism." Perhaps then, ironically enough, the cinematic theater and its cinematic stage, while relying heavily on technology and actors, can be called the "neorealism" of the theater.

Notes

1. Wim Wenders, *Emotion Pictures*, trans. Michael Hofmann (London: Faber and Faber, 1989), viii.

2. This is a favorite subject of both the writer Jack Kerouac as well as the filmmaker Wim Wenders.

3. Jean Baudrillard, *America*, trans. Chris Turner, (New York: Verso, 1988), 1.

4. Cinema comes from *cinematograph*, [Gr. *kinema*, motion, and *graphein*, to write]. *Webster's New and Universal Unabridged Dictionary*, 2nd ed., 1983, s.v. "cinema."

5. Baudrillard discusses the concept of the hyperreal in his essay, "Symbolic Exchange and Death," in Jean Baudrillard, *Selected Writings*, ed. Mark Poster (Stanford, Ca.: Stanford University Press, 1988), 143–46.

6. Baudrillard, *America*, 2.

7. Baudrillard, *America*, 2.

8. Baudrillard, *America*, .5.

9. Baudrillard, *America*, 21.

10. Baudrillard, *America*, 21.

11. Marjorie Perloff, *Radical Artifice* (Chicago: University of Chicago Press, 1991).

12. For an overview of this movement, see Richard Macksey and Eugenio Donato, eds., *The Structuralist Controversy* (Baltimore: Johns Hopkins University Press, 1970).

13. David A. Cook, *A History of Narrative Film, 3rd Edition* (New York: W.W. Norton & Company, 1996), Chapter 13.

14. Bonnie Marranca, *The Theatre of Images* (New York: Theatre Communication Group, 1972), ix.

15. Marranca, *The Theatre of Images*, x–xi.

16. Marranca, *The Theatre of Images*, x.

17. Marranca, *The Theatre of Images*, xii.

18. Richard Foreman, in discussion with the author, New York, June 2001.

19. Richard Foreman, in discussion with the author, New York, June 2001.

20. As a child, Wilson had a stutter. At seventeen he was cured by a dance instructor, Miss Byrd Hoffman, who taught him how to slow down his speech, and alleviate his body-tension through dance movements. See Laurence Shyer, *Robert Wilson and His Collaborators* (New York: Theatre Communication Group, 1989), xvi.

21. The "school" was largely responsible for promoting and launching Wilson and his work. It remained active until 1975, at which point it became only a producing organization.

22. Laurence Shyer, *Robert Wilson and His Collaborators* (New York: Theatre Communication Group, 1989), 23.

23. Shyer, *Robert Wilson and His Collaborators*, 79.

24. This is a concept that Peter Brook explored while in Iran with the poet Ted Hughes, and that later Andrei Serban also explored using original Greek texts and sounds. See Andrei Serban, "Life as a Sound," *The Drama Review* 72, (1976): 25–26.

25. Ruth Maleczech, a former actress of *Mabou Mines*, has compared Wilson's mastery of lights—his grand forté—to a plane upon which he walks and draws.

26. Glass's music, with its repetitive tones and notes, echoes Wilson's repetitive motions and abstractions.

27. See Bertolt Brecht's essay on opera, "The Modern Theatre Is the Epic Theatre," in *Brecht on Theatre,* trans. and ed. John Willett (New York: Hill and Wang, 1964), 33–42.

28. I followed the evolution of this production closely, as Wilson's American Repertory Theater (ART) assistant was a close friend and colleague, and we would have regular discussions about Wilson's approach and process for the play.

29. Wilson has mastered the art of stage motion and action to the highest degree of accuracy, a task that was firmly established to the split-second by Bertolt Brecht years before Wilson began. However, as an *auteur*-director, Wilson sometimes dehumanizes his actors and turns them into marionettes, for example, by assigning them numbers, rather than using their proper names.

30. The "knee plays" have become a permanent part of Wilson's stage vocabulary. He frequently uses them in other productions as well.

31. Shyer, *Robert Wilson and His Collaborators,* 117–18.

32. Heiner Müller, in discussion with the author, May 1991.

33. Heiner Müller, in discussion with the author, May 1991.

34. Coming from the Brechtian epic theater tradition, in which the narrative is presented in a linear manner, Müller reacts to Brecht by writing with fragments of texts from a variety of sources. Taking the helix as its form, the "synthetic fragment" weaves multiple topics, themes, and historical and political references in a concise and poetic manner. Müller's play *Hamletmachine* is only five pages long, but it is saturated with signs and references in a highly dense but poetic manner. Calling it "the shrunken head of Hamlet," Müller uses Hamlet as the basis of his synthetic fragment, through which he then weaves and creates a multiple helix using references from Shakespeare, Dostoevsky, the Hungarian revolution, Karl Marx, Mao, Lenin, current consumer society, and many others.

35. Shyer, *Robert Wilson and His Collaborators,* 123.

36. Shyer, *Robert Wilson and His Collaborators,* 123.

37. Shyer, *Robert Wilson and His Collaborators,* 122–23.

38. Shyer, *Robert Wilson and His Collaborators,* 122–23.

39. Shyer, *Robert Wilson and His Collaborators,* 123.

40. A "museum of memories" is a notion I borrow from e.e. cummings' poem, "[it is so long since my heart has been with yours]," in Richard Ellmann and Robert O'Clair, eds., *The Norton Anthology of Modern Poetry* (New York: W.W. Norton & Company, 1973), 534. The audience's memory of the production, however, is Peter Brook's "acid test of the theatre." In the Peter Brook's *The Empty Space* (New York: Atheneum, 1968), 136:

I know of one acid test in the theatre. It is literally an acid test. When a performance is over, what remains? Fun can be forgotten, but powerful emotion also disappears and good arguments lose their thread. When emotion and argument are harnessed to a wish from the audience to see more clearly into itself—then something in the mind burns. The event scorches on to the memory an outline, a taste, a trace, a smell—a picture. It is the play's central image that remains, its silhouette, and if the elements are rightly blended this silhouette will be its meaning, this shape will be the essence of what it has to say. When years later I think of a striking theatrical experience I find a kernel engraved on my memory: two tramps under a tree, an old woman dragging a cart, a sergeant dancing, three people on a sofa in hell—or occasionally a trace deeper than any imagery. I haven't a hope of remembering the meanings precisely, but from the kernel I can construct a set of meanings.

41. Richard Foreman, in discussion with the author, New York, June 2001.

42. My thanks to Carl Weber for this definition of the *verfremdungseffekt*.

43. Richard Foreman, in discussion with the author, New York, June 2001.

44. Richard Foreman, in discussion with the author, New York, June 2001.

45. Richard Foreman, in discussion with the author, New York, June 2001.

46. Richard Foreman, interview with Ken Jordan #1, January 1990. Biography of Richard Foreman, http://www.ontological.com (5 May 2002).

47. Richard Foreman, interview with Ken Jordan #1, January 1990. Biography of Richard Foreman, http://www.ontological.com (5 May 2002).

48. Richard Foreman, interview with Ken Jordan #1, January 1990. Biography of Richard Foreman, http://www.ontological.com (5 May 2002).

49. Richard Foreman, interview with Ken Jordan #1, January 1990. Biography of Richard Foreman, http://www.ontological.com (5 May 2002).

50. See Gerald Rabkin, "Don Juan," in *Richard Foreman: Art + Performance*, ed. Gerald Rabkin (Baltimore: Johns Hopkins University Press), 1999.

51. Rabkin, *Richard Foreman: Art+Performance*.

52. Richard Foreman, in discussion with the author, New York, June 2001.

53. Richard Foreman, in discussion with the author, New York, June 2001.

54. Richard Foreman, interview with Ken Jordan #1, January 1990. Biography of Richard Foreman, http://www.ontological.com (5 May 2002).

55. Richard Foreman, in discussion with the author, New York, June 2001.

56. Richard Foreman, in discussion with the author, New York, June 2001.

57. Richard Foreman, in discussion with the author, New York, June 2001.

58. Richard Foreman, interview with Ken Jordan #1, January 1990. Biography of Richard Foreman, http://www.ontological.com (5 May 2002).

59. Richard Foreman, interview with Ken Jordan #1, January 1990. Biography of Richard Foreman, http://www.ontological.com (5 May 2002).

60. Richard Foreman, interview with Ken Jordan #2, January 1990. Biography of Richard Foreman, http://www.ontological.com (5 May 2002).

61. Richard Foreman, interview with Ken Jordan #2, January 1990. Biography of Richard Foreman, http://www.ontological.com (5 May 2002).

62. Richard Foreman, interview with Ken Jordan #2, January 1990. Biography of Richard Foreman, http://www.ontological.com (5 May 2002).

63. Richard Foreman, interview with Ken Jordan #2, January 1990. Biography of Richard Foreman, http://www.ontological.com (5 May 2002).

64. "Off-Broadway's Most Inventive Directors Talk about Their Art: Discussion with Elizabeth Le Compte," in *Richard Foreman: Art+Performance*, ed. Gerald Rabkin (Baltimore: Johns Hopkins University Press), 1999, 139.

65. When asked what he would call his work, he responded that although he has a love-hate relationship with the theater, he still comes from the theater, and he still would call his work *theater*. Richard Foreman, in discussion with the author, New York, June 2001.

66. Richard Foreman, interview with Ken Jordan #1, January 1990. Biography of Richard Foreman, http://www.ontological.com (5 May 2002).

67. Richard Foreman, interview with Ken Jordan #1, January 1990. Biography of Richard Foreman, http://www.ontological.com (5 May 2002).

68. Richard Foreman, interview with Ken Jordan #1, January 1990. Biography of Richard Foreman, http://www.ontological.com (5 May 2002).

69. Richard Foreman, in discussion with the author, New York, June 2001.

70. Richard Foreman, interview with Ken Jordan #1, January 1990. Biography of Richard Foreman, http://www.ontological.com (5 May 2002).

71. Richard Foreman, in discussion with the author, New York, June 2001.

72. Heiner Müller, in discussion with the author, May 1991.

73. Heiner Müller, in discussion with the author, May 1991.

74. Richard Foreman, interview with Ken Jordan #1, January 1990. Biography of Richard Foreman, http://www.ontological.com (5 May 2002).

75. Richard Foreman, in discussion with the author, New York, June 2001.

76. Richard Foreman, in discussion with the author, New York, June 2001.

Chapter 2
Space and Structure

I would have to write a dissertation, to examine myself from top to bottom, to look at myself with ridiculous pettiness—and then? I'm sure I still won't manage to isolate everything that went into composing that single unique frame, still wouldn't succeed in pulling out, in reconstructing that unreachable indescribable mysterious component which brings everything together at the end apart from my logic, my premise, good will, talent, artistic sense. I could never succeed in dissecting that moment of magnetic fusion which gives unity and credibility to the whole kaboodle while still retaining the illusion, the seductiveness, the symbolism, of the fantasized image.

—Federico Fellini[1]

Spatial Transfiguration

The Panoptic Space

Consider Michel Foucault's description of Jeremy Bentham's *Panopticon*, a model for a prison:

> Bentham's Panopticon is the architectural figure of this composition. We know the principle on which it is based: at the periphery, an annular building; at the center, a tower; this tower is pierced with wide windows that open onto the inner side of the ring; the peripheric building is divided into cells, each of which extends the whole width of the building; they have two windows, one on the inside, corresponding to the windows of the tower; the other, on the outside, allows the light to cross the cell from one end to the other. All that is needed, then, is to place a supervisor in a central tower and to shut up in each cell a madman, a patient, a condemned man, a worker or a schoolboy. By the effect of back lighting, one can observe from the tower, standing out precisely against the light, the small captive shadows in the cells of the periphery. They are like so many cages, so many small theaters, in which each actor is alone, perfectly individualized and constantly visi-

ble. The panoptic mechanism arranges spatial unites that make it possible to see constantly and to recognize immediately. In short, it reverses the principle of the dungeon; or rather of its three functions—to enclose, to deprive of light and to hide—it preserves only the first and eliminates the other two. Full lighting and the eye of a supervisor capture better than darkness, which ultimately protected. Visibility is a trap.[2]

This description of the Panopticon resembles the theater in its spatial and "performative" nature. It is the theater in as far as it is a space that hosts the spectator and contains many actors, each with their own unique stories and plays. The entire event is illuminated with bright lights. Going even a step further, as in the theater, the actors within this space deliver their lines and perform to a spectator while being blinded by a light that is shed on them. It matters very little if the auditorium is full or not. They cannot see and even if they could, what difference would it make in their performance? The show must go on, and regardless of who is in the auditorium, they must do their best. Foucault continues: "Each individual, in his place, is securely confined to a cell from which he is seen from the front by the supervisor; but the side walls prevent him from coming into contact with his companions. He is seen, but he does not see; he is the object of information, never a subject of communication."[3]

The primary function of the Panopticon is to induce in the inmate a state of consciousness and permanent visibility that assures the automatic functioning of power—a power that brings to light and enables the spectacle to continue automatically, while the spectator can observe or sleep, as he or she wishes. In view of this, Bentham laid down the principle that power, within the Panopticon, should be at once visible and unverifiable. "Visible: the inmate will constantly have before his eyes the tall outline of the central tower from which he is spied upon. Unverifiable: the inmate must never know whether he is being looked at any one moment; but he must be sure that he may always be so."[4] The source of the panoptic power is the theater power, namely the spectator. Just as in the theater—where a spectacle cannot exist independent of its spectators—the Panopticon cannot function without the central observer, the permanent, twenty-four-hour spectator. "In the peripheric ring, one is totally seen, without ever seeing; in the central tower, one sees everything without ever being seen."[5]

Unlike the theater, the spectacle in the Panopticon is a permanent spectacle. It never stops, because the spectator is a permanent one. He or she is watching all the time by the very fact that the actor-prisoners are constantly lit, while he or she constantly remains hidden. Whether there are two people sitting there in the tower, or 200, or none at all, the performance goes on. Note that also under such circumstances, the actors become highly disciplined and rigorous. The rigor of the Panopticon echoes the rigor that Artaud so desperately wanted to implement in his theater, likening it to the rigor of a plague.[6] Examining this discipline and rigor in light of the plague, Foucault remarks:

This enclosed, segmented space, observed at every point, in which the individuals are interested in a fixed place, in which the slightest movements are supervised, in which all events are recorded, in which an uninterrupted work of writing links the center and the periphery, in which power is exercised without division, according to a continuous hierarchical figure, in which each individual is constantly located, examined and distributed among the living beings, the sick and the dead—all this constitutes a compact model of the disciplinary mechanism.[7]

With such a disciplinary mechanism at work, the actor-prisoners carry on performing every night. Just like the frozen actors on a cinema screen, the Panopticon actors are to perform every night to an auditorium of (non)existent audiences. The audience may be there, or it may not, but just as the screen shows the film to an empty or full space, the Panopticon stage shows its spectacle to an empty tower or a full one. Regardless of the audience, they must play within their cells—within their frames—advice that Diderot gave to his own actors inside a tableau: "Be, then, that which you are composing, that which you are playing. Don't pay attention to the spectators anymore, as if they didn't exist. Imagine that there is a great wall at the edge of the stage separating you from the auditorium. Play your roles as if the curtain had never risen."[8]

The panoptic space ensures rigor and precision, and much like the cinema, it functions independently of an audience. It functions purely by itself and for itself, with a stage that can stand on its own autonomously and behave precisely, automatically, systematically, and mechanically. "The panoptic schema makes any apparatus of power more intense: it assures its economy (in material, in personnel, in time); it assures its efficacy by its preventative character, its continuous functioning and its automatic mechanisms."[9]

Setting the prison metaphor aside, the panoptic construction is the ideal for a cinematic stage. It is a frame and screened space, lit such that the actors will never see the audience. It is designed and disciplined with rigor, and choreographed to the smallest detail. It is also a space in which the actors have no room for the audience: identical to the cinema, their audience is invisible, regardless of the auditorium and its (non)spectators, the actors must perform their roles as if to a full house. To implement such a space, however, a general assessment of the similarities and differences between the spaces of theater and cinema is necessary.

The theater space is called a stage, and it exists in an abundant variety of forms: proscenium, thrust, arena, open stage, environmental, and so on. The space enclosing the stage also varies in its degree. It can be an open space or a closed one, a black box, an auditorium, or a stadium. Its audience can be seated in any number of ways and in any number of configurations. Regardless of its shape and size, the theater space is defined by a stage and the surrounding space.

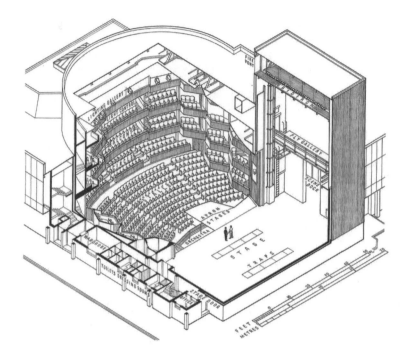

Figure 2.1. Schematic drawing of the Forum Theatre, Billingham, United Kingdom, 1968. Reprinted with permission from *Theatre and Playhouse* by Richard and Helen Leacroft, Methuen Publishing Limited, 1984.

The cinema space, on the other hand, is less variable. It consists of a single, uniform space (a black box) and a screen. Regardless of the size of the screen, the configuration is always the same: It is a screen in front of which the audience is seated. As the screen is two-dimensional—exists in R2—there can be no question of seating the audience in a round or in a thrust. The cinema space is defined by a screen and standard, parallel row seating. The cinema space is furthermore centered on the screen. It is on the screen that the audience sees the film. The screen, in return, has a singular element that enables it to contain the film: the *frame*.

The theater stage closest to that of the film screen is the proscenium theater. Whereas the cinema screen is a complete frame holding the projected image, the proscenium theater is essentially a three-quarter frame that contains the theater action. Figure 2.1 illustrates a typical proscenium stage. Here, the lower part of the frame is created by the line of the stage, and the upper part of the frame is formed by the overhang above the stage.

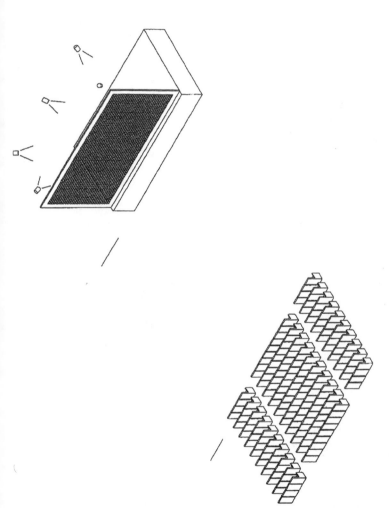

Figure 2.2. Basic schema of the cinematic theater. Hamid Arjomand, 1994.

To become a cinematic stage, the proscenium space needs to have a closure and contain a frame. And much like the cinema screen, this frame needs to contain the action of the stage within itself, such that it transforms into a *fold*, a reconception of space and time developed by Gilles Deleuze.[10] As described by Peter Eisenman, "The fold is a different kind of symbol, no longer about image or iconic representation but rather about index and mapping its own being, a mapping of its thisness in time as an event or a spectacle."[11]

Figure 2.2 illustrates the basic construction of the cinematic stage and space. Consider the proscenium theater to be constructed in such a manner that the upper and the lower lines of the frame—the optic lines that constitute the stage—are raised to create a frame at eye level, much like the cinema frame. This framed proscenium is focusing the theater event on the stage, thereby bringing it one step closer to a fold in its precision of the mapped moment. "The image must be replaced by mapping, and individuality reconceptualized in the idea of singularity . . . Singularity is not something that emerges from a ground or from a figure form. It is the quality of unfolding in time that allows the possibility of singularity. Thus the fold can never be a neutral datum; it will always be a moment if not a specific object or place in time. As such, it can be an unstable or nonstatic being in time as well as in place. The fold is neither a frame nor a figure as ground but contains elements of both."[12]

Having framed the stage of the proscenium theater, in order for the fold to be complete, the space now needs to be self-contained and autonomous. To accentuate this enclosure the frame needs a screen: a screen placed on the frame to completely isolate and enclose the space behind it. This also creates a distinct division between the spectators' and the actors' spaces. By setting this screened frame into a sufficiently distanced location, the images will be completely autonomous and self-contained. They will be a hyperreal rendition of the theater, in which no sound will escape, no light will diffuse into the spectator's space, and no life will transfer onto the other side of the screen. The screened, distanced frame will ensure that the panoptic reality is completely enclosed, autonomous, and self-contained—mirroring that of the cinema.

Much like the cinema in which the images are projected onto a framed screen, the reverse effect can be calculated in such a fold. Images are projected and represented through the screen, into the space of the audience. The screen can also be used to frame the final credits. It is on this screen that we see the film unroll, and it is on this screen that we see the credits. Just as in the cinema, the credits can be projected onto the screen of the cinematic theater. As the actors in the film do not take a bow (How could they? They are enclosed in another world, another time, space, and reality), the screen can be used to project the credits after the cinematic theater has been played and finished. The distanced frame, combined with its multipurpose screen, takes the panoptic space to a higher level, thereby creating a perfect fold capable of sustaining and maintaining a *cinematic stage*:

Place and time when no longer defined by the grid but by the fold still exist, but not as place and time in its former context, as static, figural space. This other definition of time and place involves both the simulacrum of time and place and the former reality of time and place. Narrative time is consequently altered. From here to there in space involves real time; only in mediated time, the time of film or video, can time be sped or collapsed. Today the architecture of the event must deal with both times: its former time and future time of before and after, and the media time, the time of the present that contain before and after.[13]

For the cinematic stage to exist, the event that occurs behind this fold must be in a self-sustaining and autonomous space. Behind the framed screen, the existing space—which now looks like a box or a cubicle—needs to embody the different forms of time while containing a self-sustained reality. As early as the 1970s, German set designers responded to this challenge with a feasible construction. They invented a concept of stage design that fully embodies this cinematic theater stage/space/room for the fold: the *Raum*.

The *Raum*: A Space/Room in Time and Imagination

A man, played by Marcello Mastroianni, escapes a group of women and arrives at a mansion. He enters and is greeted by a gentleman, his host. They start to talk, and he observes the architecture of the mansion. His host leaves him for a while, and Marcello parades around the space inside the mansion, observing the structure, the furniture, the lights, the room, and the new surroundings. Eventually, he stumbles upon a room within this space. He walks into the room.

This new room is a different space. It is hollow, empty, rather large, and feels like a room, but at the same time is filled with images, frames, lights, and offers another sense of space. On its walls are hundreds of large, dark slide frames with push buttons. He presses one of the buttons, and the slide frame lights up with a picture of a woman. Along with its lighting up, begins the prerecorded sound of the woman in the frame: her sexual fantasy with her sexual/sensual sounds. He presses the button again, and the frame and its sound go off. He walks down the wall and presses another frame button, and a different slide with a different light, with a different fantasy, speech, and sound starts. He presses it again, and it goes off. The scene carries on for a few minutes, thus revealing a very strange space, a very surreal-like room, which can only exist in the realm of dream and imagination. It is a space that reveals lights, life, sounds, and senses, yet manages to remain enclosed and act as a room. The man discovers that this space is the shrine of the "conquests" of his host: an inconceivable reality, an outrageous sense of imagination that can only take place in another time, space, and reality.

This is a scene from *The City of Women* (1980), a film by the architect, designer, and director Federico Fellini. This example is merely an illustration of the German design concept of *Raum*: an enclosed, architectural atmospheric location that acts as a space and relays and actualizes inconceivable concepts. The

Raum is a limited place, a site, in which one's imagination roam as far as possible. To translate the word *Raum* to "room" would reduce its "spatial" dimensions, and to translate it into "space" would lose its sense of "enclosure within another architectural setting." Thus, an English equivalent for the *Raum* does not exist. The closest would be the combined words "space/room."[14]

The *Raum* stage design has radicalized contemporary theater. It has affected playwrights, designers, and directors, and forced many to see theater in a different light. Designers have turned into directors, architects have turned into stage designers, and writers and directors have started to think in terms of spatial configurations for their texts—be it on paper, or on stage. Even a few film designers-directors, such as Fellini, have incorporated this concept into their films.

A reaction to traditional theater design concepts in which designers support the author-director's interpretation, the *Raum* emerged to give the designer complete freedom to convey his or her own response to the audience. Rather than following the director's interpretation, the *Raum*-maker also plunges into the text, inhabits it, and comes out with his or her own set of reactions, feelings, and interpretations. The designer creates the *Raum* to convey to the spectators his or her own set of reactions to and understandings of the textual world.

A designer creates an atmospheric location that represents the text and stimulates the mind and the senses. The actor, the director, and the audience all bring their own senses and sensitivity to this space/room. The *Raum*-maker fabricates the product and gives it to the director; the director is free to take it or leave it. If he or she takes it, the directorial concept will have to adjust and grow out of this newly offered world. It is a world in which the imagination can be stimulated a hundred times over, and in which lights and objects create another realm, another reality. The inhabitants will undoubtedly have conflicts and clash with their new surroundings, but they nevertheless will learn to adapt and adjust to their new lifestyle. Their new lifestyle is one in which, for example, light is no longer just a source of light, but is actually a real material as much as are the actual bodies.

The *Raum* is a spatial affirmation: a space/room that is designed independently from the action, the interpretation of the director, and the sounds of the text. The *Raum* creator, however, takes into account the design elements of light and actor's bodies in actualizing his or her atmospheric sense. Perhaps the best way to understand and fully illustrate the notion of *Raum* is to look at the works of some important *Raum* makers. The four principal designers of *Raum* are: Wilfried Minks, who was the first to actualize and introduce the *Raum* to the German stage in the 1960s and 1970s; Karl-Ernst Herrmann, who has been designing for the Schaubühne since the early 1970s; Achim Freyer, who began in the 1970s in East Berlin and has recently become a director; and finally Erich Wonder, who was Heiner Müller's preferred designer, and who has also recently become a director.

One might say the *Raum* revolution was triggered in 1969 by Wilfried Minks' design for Peter Stein's production of Goethe's *Tasso* at Theater Bremen.[15] For this production, Minks had covered the entire ground with a dark green AstroTurf. The walls were covered in a double layer: the first was a golden wall, the second layer was a circular plastic perimeter. In addition to this spatial construct, to pay homage to Goethe, Minks placed Goethe's bust onstage, which was moved to different areas for the different scenes. This design was the first of its kind. The audience had never been exposed to such a well-defined, enclosed space that, along with lights, created a compelling atmosphere throughout the production. The introduction of Minks' *Raum* into the German theater became even more well-defined when Minks created his design for Klaus Michael Grüber's *The Tempest*. Here, Minks covered the entire stage with eleven tons of sand (to create an island) and placed a gigantic fluorescent arch above the stage. With this design, Minks integrated light as a material element of the *Raum*.

Karl-Ernst Herrmann's *Raum* for Peter Stein's production of *As You Like It* was highly complex and expensive. In this design, Herrmann used multiple *Raums*. The audience walked into a white space that was divided into narrow segments and watched the action while standing up. The action took place in multiple directions and on a variety of differentiated levels. The audience was then led out through a narrow passageway into a very detailed forest with soil, a pond, trees, insects, shrubs, bushes, and the sounds of birds and forest life. Herrmann had succeeded in creating a real forest of Arden along with all its sensory elements, including the feeling of an open space within an enclosed one.

The *Raum*, in concept, can stand independently, generating atmosphere, moods, feelings, thoughts, and a narrative. Achim Freyer's *Monument to Kleist*, which was located in the lobby of the theater (while a Kleist production was taking place), consisted of a black-floored narrow cage with a shooting gallery wall. Inside, there was a coffin, dead flowers, and a dog with a collar made with butcher knives. On a box at the opposite end, a man dressed in black, with a white mask, stood on a box and took shots at the dog. Having failed at his attempts, he places the gun in his mouth and shoots himself.

In 1979, Freyer created an even more disturbing and complex *Raum* installation: his famous *Deutschland—ein Lebensraum*. The audience entered a large, white room through a low entrance. Inside, there was an exit door through which light entered, but the door was blocked by a pool of water. A hiker figure standing on a box peered through a window at a sunset and a mountain. In a corner, a Christmas tree was placed; above it were two video monitors that showed rabbits being fed, and underneath it were red cushions, puppets, a blanket, and a gramophone that played children's tunes. A section of the floor had a glass pool, underneath which a figure in a gas mask and an oxygen pump, some red hair, and fish floated. Attached to one of the walls was a glass box with a windshield wiper, which was filled with flies. The room was also divided by barbed wire with alarms, which would go off with the slightest contact. Finally, there were eight rabbits whose eyes, hearts, and genitals were painted with red paint and their ears were stamped with large swastikas.

Finally, Erich Wonder's *Raums* have created sensations in the contemporary German theater.[16] Wonder primarily uses an empty sparse space filled with lights as material. In designing Sophocles' *Antigone*, the *Raum* was nothing but a hanging gigantic cube of light, which with the shift in colors, prescribed different atmospheres. Downstage in this *Raum* was an enormous vertical windshield wiper made from a long, thin, rectangular rod of light. Each time the rod wiped the stage, the configuration and lights shifted to create another setting, mood, and atmosphere. Both scenes and actors would (dis)appear with the light wiping the front of the stage. Wonder describes the stage effect of his windshield wiper: "A huge blazing rod of light moves across the stage like a windscreen wiper, eradicating the previous scenes."[17]

Perhaps his most well-known design is for Müller's *The Task*. Here, Wonder divided the audience into two halves, by placing a long, narrow cage running through the center of the theater. Inside, a black panther paced back and forth. The proscenium stage was framed by an isosceles triangle through which the audience was forced to view the stage action. Behind this frame, Wonder had a swinging piano attached to a rope hanging from the fly gallery, real rain, harsh spot lights, and industrial sparks and fires. In this *Raum*, Müller's *The Task* was performed with actors adding to the atmosphere of the space/room by becoming wet, nude, and positioning themselves in very precise spatial locations. Müller's texts often prescribe a *Raum* for the stage and the actors. Müller remarks that Wonder's *Raums* are a challenge for him, and that (he) the director can use this challenge to add to his creative staging. "That's what all challenges are: creative."[18]

The *Raum* has certainly revolutionized our approach to performance, creating a new perspective for a "dramaturgy of images." The drawback of the design is that it is very powerful, and has the potential to overwhelm the other elements involved.[19] The *Raum* remains an autonomous art form.[20] It has not only contributed to the spatial reality of theater, but it has also contributed to its social role, giving complete freedom to the artists' imagination.

Behind the screened frame (the fold), and at a great enough distance, a *Raum* can inhabit any reality of cinematic theater, from Shakespeare to modern-day authors. For the cinematic theater to take place, its first principle needs to be cinematic space: a panoptic space constructed by a screened, distanced, and framed proscenium. It needs to be a distanced space defined by a fold and containing a *Raum*.

Within this cinematic space, the cinematic theater can produce and present its production, or what could be called a *[screen]play*. The performance time and form within this space must now be defined and examined. The answer to how such a cinematic space can present a [screen]play lies in a close examination of the film form and film structure.

Composing the Image-Narrative

The Tableau

In his essay "Diderot, Brecht, and Eisenstein," Roland Barthes begins by establishing two distinct relationships between mathematics and the arts. The first relationship is one between mathematics and acoustics, and the second is one between geometry and the theater. He writes, ". . . certainly the theatre is that practice which calculates the *observed* place of things: if I put the spectacle here, the spectator will see this; if I put it elsewhere, he won't see it and I can take advantage of that concealment to profit by the illusion."[21]

This placement of people and objects, in a Cartesian manner, is what is more commonly known in the theater as *blocking*. The author writes the scene, and the director fleshes it out on the stage by blocking it. Blocking is to the theater as a rough sketch is to a painting. It determines what the viewer sees, or rather what he should or should not see. Secondary to this blocking—this preliminary sketch—are all the other elements, such as the set, lights, colors, costumes, sound, and so forth, which when added on, yield the final image[22] we see on stage.

Barthes then continues by defining the stage, and his definition is not so far from that of Peter Brook. Brook's definition can be summarized by the following formula: empty space (stage) + a human walking across it (actor) + another watching (audience) = Theater.[23] Barthes takes it a step further, remaining more schematic and geometric: ". . . the stage is just that line which intersects the optic beam, tracing its end point and, in a sense, the inception of its development: here would be instituted, against music (the text), *representation*."[24] Barthes' theater stage is defined by the spectator and the event on stage, as is Brook's, yet the representation itself is inscribed through geometry. He continues:

> Representation is not directly defined by imitation: even if we were to get rid of the notions of "reality" and "verisimilitude" and "copy," there would still be "representation," so long as a subject (author, reader, spectator, or observer) directed his gaze towards a horizon and there projected the base of a triangle of which his eye (or the mind) would be the apex. [25]

This triangle is the essence of (artistic) visual representation. Barthes points out that all the arts—with the exception of the dioptic ones—use this trigonometry to communicate. Be it a painting, a play, a sculpture, or a film, they all use the eye of the spectator and the optic line to complete the representation. The eye acts as the triangular apex to the frame that contains the representation. Through this geometric device, all the arts project fragments to describe them: "to discourse is to paint a mental picture."[26]

Here, it is important to observe that what Barthes calls "the stage—the line which intersects the optic beam, tracing its end point, in a sense, the inception of its development" is nothing else but the line of a frame. All artistic representations exist within a closed system. This closure—this closed system that contains the artwork—is the frame. A frame, or *cadre*, (en)closes a painting; it creates a border that limits the representation to the spectator's (viewer's) eye. Without the frame, representation could not be complete, could not be closed, could not be contained, and thus could not take place.[27] The frame contains the artwork, and thereby sets the art apart from its environs. It negates what is not art—what is not included inside the frame—by prohibiting all relations with the outside.

Perhaps Kant's *parergon*, outlined in his third critique, *The Critique of Judgment* (1790), comes the closest to a philosophical definition of the frame.[28] *Parergon* is derived from the Greek words *para* = outside of, border of and *ergon* = the force, center. Jacques Derrida observes that, "What constitutes them as *parerga* is not simply their exteriority as a surplus, it is the internal structural link which rivets them to the lack in the interior of the *ergon*. And this lack would be constitutive of the very unity of the *ergon*. Without this lack, the *ergon* would have no need of a *parergon*."[29]

In other words, the frame is defined in conjunction with the inside/outside boundaries. Without the outside, the frame could not exist, and without the inside, the frame would have no purpose. Yet, the frame has a paradoxical existence in that it is forced to belong to neither the inside nor the outside. It exists on the very edge, as a border, as a protector. Derrida notes, "And when Kant, replies to our question 'What is a frame?' by saying: it's a *parergon*, a hybrid of outside and inside, but a hybrid which is not a mixture or a half-measure, an outside which is called to the inside of the inside in order to constitute it as an inside."[30]

In light of the frame, the triangular representation of which Barthes speaks could not take place if it were not for the frame. In order for the apex of the triangle to be the apex, it needs to be defined in conjunction with a limited closed line, in conjunction with the frame. If the frame contains the work of art, then the eye (apex) can use the frame to create its triangular representation.

The frame also defines the *tableau*. An immediate example is a painting: the painting is enclosed within its frame. The frame is a border with limits that enclose the image, which is the representation created by paint on canvas. Yet, an important aspect of the frame lies in its own self-limit, in its subtlety. With a frame that is too massive, the artwork will lose its position and value; with a frame that is too invisible, the artwork will lose its differentiation between the inside and the outside. The frame remains an important definition of the tableau-artwork. Without it, a painting, a staged scene, or a shot in a film—a tableau of any kind—could not exist. Together, the frame and its contents (the artwork) define the tableau in theatrical, pictorial, literary, cinematic, or other forms of art.

The exact origin of the word tableau is unclear. As early as the eighteenth century, in "A Notion of the Historical Draught or the Judgment of Hercules" (1712), Anthony Cooper, Earl of Shaftesbury, writes:

> Before we enter on the examination of our historical sketch, it may be proper to remark, that by the word Tablature (for which we have yet no name in English, besides the general one of picture) we denote, according to the original word Tabula, a work not only distinct from a mere portraiture, but from all the wilder sorts of painting which are in a manner absolute and independent [i.e., not subject to the demand for unity]; such as the paintings in fresco upon the walls, the ceilings, the staircases, the cupolas, and other remarkable places of either churches or palaces.[31]

He continues:

> But it is then that in painting we may give any particular work the name of tablature, when the work is in reality 'a single piece, comprehended in one view, and formed according to one single intelligence, meaning, or design; which constitutes a real whole, by a mutual and necessary relation of its parts, the same as of the members in a natural body.'[32]

To illustrate and clarify the notion of the tableau, consider the following definitions of border, tableau, and frame:

bor•der *n* [ME *bordure*, fr. MF, fr. OF, fr. *border* to border, fr. *bort* border, of Gmc origin; akin to OE *bord*] (14c) **1** : an outer part of edge **2** : an ornamental design at the edge of a fabric or rug **3** : a narrow bed of planted ground along the edge of a garden or walk <a ~ of tulips> **4** : BOUNDARY <crossed the ~ into Italy> **5** : a plain or decorative margin around printed matter

tab•leau *n*, *pl* tab•leaux *also* tableaus [F, fr. MF *tablel*, dim. of *table,* fr. OF] (1699) **1** : a graphic description or representation: PICTURE <winsome *tableaux* of old-fashioned literary days and ways —J. D. Hart> **2** : a striking or artistic grouping **3** : [short for *tableau vivant* (fr. F, lit., living picture)]: a depiction of a scene usu. presented on a stage by silent and motionless costumed participants

frame *n* (14c) **1 a** : something composed of parts fitted together and united **b**: the physical makeup of an animal and esp. a human body: PHYSIQUE, FIGURE **2 a** : the constructional system that gives shape or strength (as to a building); *also* : a frame dwelling **b** : such a skeleton not filled in or covered **3** *obs* : the act or manner of framing **4 a** : a machine built upon or within a framework <a spinning ~> **b** : an open case or structure made for admitting, enclosing, or supporting something <a window ~> . . .[33]

Having examined the definitions of the tableau and the frame, the important role of the tableau in Barthes' essay becomes even more illuminated. Barthes continues his essay by pointing out that the notion of tableau is central for the eighteenth-century French philosopher and writer Denis Diderot (1713–1784). Though Diderot was the first to centralize this concept, the tableau quickly became a primary notion in the field of aesthetics. Its importance has carried over to twentieth-century aesthetics, where it has played an important role in both the epic theater of Bertolt Brecht (1898–1956) and the montage theory of Sergei Mikhailovich Eisenstein (1898–1948). Barthes examines the role of the tableau in all three of these theoreticians and innovators.

He begins with Diderot, whose aesthetic "is based on the identification of the theatrical scene and the pictorial tableau: the perfect play will be a series of tableaux, i.e., a gallery, a salon: the stage offers the spectator 'as many real tableaux as there are, in the action, moments which favor the painter.' " [34] The perfect play is one that only shows the audience the correct number of paintings. The "correct number" is the essential minimum that is needed to communicate the thought or images behind a narrative. The best parallel is that of a gallery. Within a gallery, not every painting of an artist can be displayed; each and every painting must therefore be carefully selected for the exposition. For the purpose of clarity, this selection is called "External Composition," "Sequencing," or "Selection B."

As for the tableau itself, it needs to be well defined. "The [pictorial, theatrical, literary] tableau is a pure projection, sharp-edged, incorruptible, irreversible, which banishes into nothingness everything around it, which is therefore unnamed, and promotes to the status of essence, to light, to sight, everything it brings into its field." [35] This is the task of the painter. He or she needs to select what to paint, what to focus on, and what to bring into light. In contrast to the previous selection—Selection B, Sequencing, or External Composition—made by the gallery curator, or the slide show creator, this selection is made by the painter or photographer. This selection determines what enters the frame and what does not, and is thus the Internal Selection, or the first set of selection, "Selection A." On a canvas, limited by the frame, the painter cannot simultaneously place the emphasis on the outside landscape and the inside architecture, unless it is a cubist painting. The painter needs to select and limit his or her choices carefully. Thus, the essence of the tableau is based on the frame. What the painter selects and brings into his or her frame becomes the tableau. This Selection A, which defines the tableau, takes place long before the sequence and presentation of the tableaux in a gallery and saloon—that is, long before Selection B.

Whatever representation it may be—pictorial, theatrical, or literary—the internal composition (Selection A) frames the image and creates the tableau. It consciously imposes well-defined borders on the image. These borders act as geometrical perimeters, defining the limits and space of the tableau. The tableau cannot extend beyond the frame—or rather beyond *its* frame. The frame is placed around the tableau to enclose it, limit it, and forbid any interaction with the outside. Thanks to its frame, the tableau becomes a defined and a self-contained entity. It becomes a "pure projection" with "sharp edges;" it is "incorruptible" and "irreversible," thus a tableau. This is the case for scenes that are staged in the theater.

Diderot's emphasis on the tableau foreshadows the necessity of a director—a *metteur-en-scène*—and the task of staging, or *mise-en-scène*. In his early writings of the 1750s and 1760s, particularly the *Entretiens sur le Fils Naturel* (1757) and the *Discours de la poésie dramatique* (1758), Diderot was already relating his notion of the tableau to the theater, and thereby calling for *mise-en-scène*. In these early writings, Diderot challenged painters to paint a scene, in one instant and in such a manner that would be more convincing than the theater could represent. In the same way, he encouraged playwrights to give up their surprises and *coups de théâtre* in favor of the tableau.

In *Entretiens sur le Fils Naturel*, for example, he distinguishes between the two as follows: "An unforeseen incident that takes place in the action, and which subtly changes the state of the characters, is a *coup de théâtre*. A blocking of these characters on the stage, so natural and so true, that is rendered faithfully by a painter, and that would please me on canvas, is a tableau."[36]

Here, Diderot suggests that the stage composition of the tableau is more important than eventful ruptures and surprises. The tableau can have a stage-composition or blocking with life of its own, independent of additional effects. Elsewhere he writes: "One must . . . leave these *coups de théâtre*, whose effects are momentary, and instead find tableaux. The more one sees a beautiful tableau, the more it will become pleasing."[37] The *coups de théâtre* is seen as a cheap trick that is perhaps the equivalent of our contemporary special effect, while the tableau is a "visually satisfying, essentially silent, *seemingly* accidental groupings of figures, which if properly managed were capable of moving the audience to the depths of its collective being" (emphasis my own).[38]

"Seemingly" is emphasized, as all gestures, all blockings, and all movements are carefully selected by the director. After all, the director is the *metteur-en-scène*, or the one who "places things on stage. "No choice should be arbitrary, but rather should follow from the basic rules of logic and composition. This being the case, the composition must seem natural on stage and not contrived. In his *Pensées détachées*, Diderot writes: "A composition must be rendered such that it will convince me that it could be rendered in no other way; a figure must act or rest so as to persuade me that it could be done in no other way."[39] Thus, in the internal composition (Selection A), every gesture and blocking should be selected and composed, but not forced onto the tableau or the audiences' eyes. The final composition must be logical, natural, and seemingly pleasant to the spectator.[40]

In all tableaux, it is of primary importance that the internal composition renders, communicates, and represents the narrative (or image) to its spectators in the most clear and pleasurable manner. The internal composition must have its own logic such that it does not confuse the viewer, but rather invites them to enjoy and comprehend with pleasure. After all, it was Brecht himself who, with all his belief in educating the audience through theater and with all his didactic plays, maintained that theater should first and foremost retain its element of

pleasure. In Section 3 of his "A Short Organum for the Theatre," Brecht pro-
claims: "From the first time it has been the theatre's business to entertain people, as it also has of all the other arts. It is this business which always gives it
its particular dignity; it needs no other passport than fun, but this it has got to
have."[41]

In *Absorption and Theatricality*, Michael Fried ties in this relationship
between the audience-pleasure-tableaux, by pointing out that:

> For Diderot and his colleagues, the painter's task was above all to reach
> the beholder's soul by way of his eyes. The traditional formulation was
> amplified by another, which like the first was widely shared: a painting, it
> was claimed, had first to attract (*attirer, appeler*) and then to arrest (*ar-
> rêter*) and finally to enthrall (*attacher*) the beholder, that is, a painting
> had to call to someone, bring him to a halt, in front of itself, and hold him
> there as if spell bound and unable to move.[42]

Referring to a more contemporary form of image, Roland Barthes argues
Diderot's point for the image in photography. For Barthes, the image contained
in the frame of a photograph must contain two essential characteristics: the *studium*, which behaves as the cerebral element of the image, or that which leads
the viewer to understand the historical, social, or political aspect of the photograph, and the *punctum*, which will pierce, puncture, and disrupt the stadium,
thereby pulling in the audience in a guttural manner.[43] Regardless of the medium—literary, theatrical, photographic, or cinematic—the image within the
frame is capable of containing both the *studium* as well as the *punctum*, and
therefore, it needs to be well composed before presented to its audience.

As for the external selection (Selection B), Diderot wanted his theater audience to watch the scenes or tableaux much like the audience of a painting gallery. "The spectator in the theatre," he maintained, "should be thought of as
before a canvas, or before a diverse selection of tableaux that follow one another
as if by magic."[44] The word "magic" evokes Artaud, who of course did not arrive on the scene until much later. It is important to note that Diderot was fully
aware of what Artaud later would name "the language of the theatre." He was
aware of the importance of silences, stillness, gestures, and movement, how
they can be used in the tableaux, and how they can have a powerful impact on
their spectators, perhaps even more than speech and words can. As early as
1751, in his surreal description of Lady Macbeth's sleepwalk, Diderot points
out this language of the theater and its force:

> There are sublime gestures, which all oratory eloquence can never express.
> Such is the case in Macbeth, one of Shakespeare's tragedies. The sleepwalk-
> ing Macbeth, in silence and with eyes closed, walks forwards on stage, imi-
> tating the actions of a person who is washing her hands, as if they were her
> own hands still stained with the blood of her king . . . I am not aware of any-
> thing so moving in speech as the silence and movements of the hands of
> this lady. What an image of remorse![45]

Internal Composition/Internal Construct: The *Gestus*

Gesture is perhaps the most fundamental notion of composition in the theater. What cannot be expressed by words can be demonstrated through gestures; what can be said in words can be supplemented through gestures. In silence, that which is taking place on stage is completely communicated and represented through the language of gestures. Gestures are at the heart of every human interaction and every human thought, feeling, and communication. Where there are human interactions, there will also be gestures. By the same token, as it is a human art, theater will then have gesture as its language of stage. Gesture is also the language of films and cinema. It is what is located at the heart of every visual tableau. Barthes observes the importance of the gesture through his examination of the tableau. He examines the inside of the frame and the contents of the tableau: What is it inside, at the heart of the frame, which makes the tableau possible? What makes a "perfect" tableau perfect? What is being framed and how is it done to make it into a special moment—what Doris Lessing calls the "pregnant moment"? How is the canvas, the stage, the photograph, or the film shot framed to yield the maximum amount of communication? For example, as Barthes relates,

> The painter possesses only one moment: the one he will immobilize on canvas; hence, he must choose this moment well, affording it in advance the greatest possible yield of meaning and of pleasure: necessarily total, this moment will be artificial (unreal: this is not realist art), it will be a hi-eroglyph in which can be read at a glance (in single apprehension, if we turn to the theatre, to the cinema) the present, the past, and the future, i.e., the historical meaning of the represented gesture."[46]

The key words here are "hieroglyph" and "artificial time." *Artificial time* is time that is condensed (as in Chekhov) or elongated (as in Wilson and Glass). What matters is that the chosen moment fully represents its content within the given time. The chosen instant has an instant to communicate all that it contains: the past, the present, and the future. Within a single moment, that which is within the *cadre* [the frame] needs to act as if it were a hieroglyph. Regardless of the chosen moment, the hieroglyph has only an instant to represent and communicate itself to the eye of the spectator. In this respect, this representation, abstract or concrete, must be carefully composed and planned to yield the maximum result, a so-called pregnant moment. "This crucial moment, totally concrete and totally abstract, is what Lessing will call (in *Laocoön*) the *pregnant moment*."[47]

The pregnant moment need not be limited to the painting tableau. It equally exists where there is a frame and a representation, that is, in theater and cinema. In the same manner that a painter has an instant at his disposal to represent (paint) on his canvas, the theater director has an instant to represent (stage) on his stage, and a filmmaker has an instant to compose (shoot) his image within the frame (the shot). In each case, a highly significant gesture is framed. This highly significant gesture is what renders a regular moment a "pregnant moment."

Not every gesture is significant, however. The significance arrives when the gesture takes on a social or political meaning and something is revealed. In discussing the concept of *Gestus*, Carl Weber, assistant director to Brecht from 1952–56, points out, "Eventually, *Gestus* became to be understood by Brecht, as far as the actor is concerned (there are other applications of the concept, but we are talking about the actor here), as the total process, the "ensemble" of all physical behavior the actor displays when showing us a character on stage by way of his/her social interactions."[48]

For example, there is nothing significant about a man chasing flies; it is neither social nor political, nor does it reveal anything. Yet, place the same man in rags, and the gesture will reveal the misery of poverty. To take another example, a hand pressing down on someone's head can be a gesture of oppression, but place some diamond rings on the hand, and dress the oppressed in rags, and now the gesture will have a significance of the rich oppressing the poor. To take other examples: a man and a women walk by each other and suddenly their eyes meet, they stop and smile, and turn away shyly—this can be a gesture of love; a child placed at the center of a circle, about to be pulled apart by two so-called mothers, can be a gesture for justice; and so on. Figure 2.3 shows director Liviu Ciulei demonstrating a small, but critical *Gestus*. A simple hand gesture can mean many things, depending upon the context.

Figure 2.3. Liviu Ciulei demonstrating *Gestus* to actors. *Squabbles in Chiogga*, Carlo Goldoni, New York University, 1989.

The gestures all have weight that carries a meaning unto themselves and by themselves; these gestures are what create pregnant moments, both in paintings as well as in the theater and cinema. Barthes observes: "Brecht's theatre, Eisenstein's cinema are sequences of pregnant moments: when Mother Courage bites the coin the recruiting sergeant offers her and, because of this tiny interval of mistrust, loses her son, she demonstrates both her past as a tradeswoman and the future in store for her: all her children dead because of her moneymaking blindness."[49] This heavy gesture, embedded with a social meaning and responsible for the creation of the pregnant moment, is what Brecht defines more precisely as the "*Gestus*." In an essay titled "On Gestic Music," Brecht writes:

Not all gests are social gests. The attitude of chasing away a fly is not yet a social gest, though the attitude of chasing away a dog may be one, for instance if it comes to represent a badly dressed man's continual battle against watchdogs. One's efforts to keep one's balance on a slippery surface result in a social gest as soon as falling down would mean 'losing face'; in other words, losing one's market value. The gest of working is definitely a social gest, because all human activity directed towards the mastery of nature is a social undertaking, an undertaking between men.[50]

Ultimately, the *Gestus* is tied to human relationships, and as human relationships are the basis of theater and most of cinema, *Gestus* is at the heart of their frame. Brecht relates the *Gestus* with his general philosophy of the theater: "The main subject of the drama must be relationships between one man and another as they exist today, and that is what I'm primarily concerned to investigate and find means of expression for."[51] Later in "A Short Organum for the Theatre," he reaffirms this point:

The realm of attitudes adopted by the characters towards one another is what we call the realm of gest. Physical attitude, tone of voice and facial expression are all determined by a social gest: the characters are cursing, flattering, instructing one another, and so on. The attitudes which people adopt towards one another include even those attitudes which would appear to be quite private such as the utterances of physical pain in an illness, or of religious faith. These expressions of a gest are usually highly complicated and contradictory, so that they cannot be rendered by any single word and the actor must take care that in giving his image the necessary emphasis he does not lose anything, but emphasizes the entire complex.[52]

The bold stroke of paint that creates the gesture on canvas also brings with it the sharper, more subtle, and finer strokes and gestures. The theater, as well as the cinema, cannot do away with the *Gestus*. It is there from the opening until the closing. With respect to observing the *Gestus* moment by moment of every second, there needs to be a director who can choreograph as well as direct and adjust his actors' attitudes and gestures because "a theatre where everything depends on the gest cannot do without choreography."[53] In addition, "The actor masters his character by paying critical attention to its manifold utterances, as also to those of his counterparts and of all the other characters involved," and "splitting such material into one gest after another, the actor masters his character by first mastering the story."[54]

Here, we arrive at the central notion for both the theater as well as the cinema: the story. "Everything hangs on the 'story'; it is the heart of the theatrical performance. . . . The 'story' is the theatre's great operation, the complete fitting together of all the basic incidents, embracing the communications and impulses that must now go to make up the audience's entertainment."[55] We have seen that the theater narrative works by a series of pregnant tableaux and that inside every frame, every tableau, there is a *Gestus* of some kind that gives the tableau its pregnant moment. We have also seen that through the *Gestus*, the tableau aims to convey, communicate, and please the spectator in the best possible manner. In section 66 of the Organum, Brecht reaffirms this point:

> Each single incident has its basic gest: Richard Gloster courts his victim's widow. The Child's true mother is found by means of a chalk circle. God has a bet with the Devil for Dr. Faustus' soul. Woyzeck buys a cheap knife in order to do his wife in, etc. The grouping of the characters on the stage and the movements of the groups must be such that the necessary beauty is attained above all by elegance with which the material conveying that gest is set out and laid bare to the understanding of the audience.[56]

The next question becomes: How is the story presented to the audience? Given the fact that the image-narrative is constructed primarily through the *Gestus* and the tableau in its form, how is it presented the audience? How is the narrative structured?

The [Cinematic and Epic] Structure

In an essay titled "The Modern Theatre Is the Epic Theatre," Brecht answers these questions by drawing out a chart explaining and illuminating the difference between "Dramatic Theatre" and his own so-called "Epic Theatre."[57] Looking at the chart closely, we find a segment regarding the narrative or story (emphasis in italics is my own):

DRAMATIC THEATRE	EPIC THEATRE
eyes on the finish	eyes on the course
one scene makes another	each scene for itself
growth	*montage*
linear development	in curves

We can note here that as early as 1930, Brecht was using the term "montage" to describe his narrative structure for the epic theater. Though he does not give us an exact definition of what montage really is, he gives us enough clues to construct our own definition. To begin with, montage is the opposite of "growth." It moves "in curves," has no "linear development," and lets each scene speak for itself, standing on its own. We can find Brecht's best definition of "montage"—without the word being used even once!—in "A Short Organum for the Theatre." In relation to how the actor ought to build his or her role, Brecht dictates that the actor ought to learn his or her part through the story. Specifically, the actor should learn his or her part through the story in a process of montage. In other words, the learning should be in sections, fragment by fragment, gest by gest, part by part, and not in an orderly fashion or in a linear manner. Rather, it should be through skipping and hopping around from one section to another, from one episode to another. Through this process, the actor can fully understand the complexities of his or her character through other episodes and relations. Metaphorically, the actor can learn his or her role through the narrative, through a process resembling a jigsaw puzzle. Brecht writes:

> Splitting such material into one gest after another, the actor masters his character by first mastering the 'story'. It is only after walking all around the entire episode that he can, as it were by a single leap, seize and fix his character, complete with all its individual features. Once he has done his best to let himself be amazed by the inconsistencies in its various attitudes, knowing that he will in turn have to make them amaze the audience, then the story as a whole gives him a chance to pull the inconsistencies together; for the story, being a limited episode, has a specific sense, i.e. only gratifies a specific fraction of all the interests that could rise.[58]

The epic structure is similar to the cinematic structure because it is a structure like a jigsaw puzzle, with every scene presenting and unveiling a new part of the story, each able to stand on its own. It is a structure with an implicit, built-in montage system. Barthes points this out in examining both Brecht's epic theater and Eisenstein's filmmaking. He illuminates the structure by pointing out that both are based on a series or sequence of tableaux (Selection B), and that the tableaux are carefully set scenes, as we say a table is "set" (Selection A):

> Brecht indicated early that in the epic theatre (which proceeds by successive tableaux) the entire burden of the meaning and of pleasure is conveyed by each scene, not by the whole; on the level of the play, no development, no ripening; an ideal meaning of course (on the level of each scene, each tableau), but no final meaning, nothing but projections, each of which possesses a sufficient demonstrative power.[59]

This epic theater structure, as defined and implemented by Bertolt Brecht, is akin to the cinematic structure.

In section 67 of "A Short Organum," Brecht writes about the epic structure: "As we cannot invite the audience to fling itself into a story as if it were a river and let itself be carried vaguely hither and thither, the individual episodes have to be knotted together in such a way that the knots are easily noticed. The episodes must not succeed one another indistinguishably but must give us a chance to interpose our judgment."[60] We cannot, therefore, go for a swim; theater is more a game of hopscotch, where the stage offers to us, the spectators, different tableaux, one by one, and apart from one another.

The story, within the epic construction, thus unfolds tableau by tableau (scene by scene) with each tableau remaining independent of the previous one. The narrative structure remains linear, with emphasis placed on each individual tableau. Tableau by tableau, the play moves forward, tableau by tableau the narrative unfolds, and tableau by tableau the momentum transfers up to the end. This is the epic structure:

$$[\,]\,[\,]\,[\,]\,[\,]\,[\,]\,[\,]\,[\,]\,[\,]\,[\,]\,[\,]\,[\,]\,[\,]\,[\,]$$

"The parts of the story have to be carefully set off one against another by giving each its own structure as a play within a play."[61] In this light, the epic structure is purely dependent on its external selection of its tableaux (Selection B). A good analogy is that of a person going through a long corridor of an art gallery to see a photography exhibit on a specific topic. Each photo has its own story, its own narrative, and stands framed on its own, independent of others. Once the viewer is done with it, he moves on to the next photos. Though the photos are all independent of one another, together—as the sum of all the images and photographs in the exposition—they construct the narrative pertinent to the theme. A more refined analogy would be a slide show: the person sits in a seat and watches the (linear) series of photographic slides that are being presented. The advantage, of course, is that in a gallery—or in a slide show—moving back is a possibility. In the theater, such is not the case. The audience cannot rewind to a previous scene (except during rehearsal).

To explain the previous diagram, it is enough to look at the structure of a late Brecht play (epic vs. didactic), such as *The Caucasian Chalk Circle*. The play is structured with tableaux in two parts in the following manner:

Prologue [0]
PART I: [1] [2] [3]
PART II: [1] [2]

To add further precision and focus for every tableau, Brecht—like the painter and the photographer—names each of his tableaux. The titles also need to reflect the essence of the tableau; they have to reflect the center of what is being framed.[62]

Barthes continues by pointing out that the epic structure of Brecht holds true for Eisenstein's films: "The same with Eisenstein: the film is a contiguity of episodes, each of which signifies absolutely, being aesthetically perfect. . . . This is Eisenstein's primary power: no single image is boring, we are not forced to wait for the next one in order to understand and be delighted."[63] For Barthes, Eisenstein's films, in form and structure, operate under the same principle as the plays of Brecht: They are both carefully constructed sequences of perfect (carefully composed) moments (tableaux). In both cases, Brecht and Eisenstein rely on Diderot's notion of tableau to define the structure of theater and cinema—a structure that is simple, yet complex in its internal composition and external sequencing (montage).

Notes

1. Federico Fellini, *Comments on Film*, ed. Giovanni Grazzini, trans. Joseph Henry (Fresno, Calif.: Press at California State University, 1988), 100.
2. Michel Foucault, *Discipline and Punish: The Birth of the Prison*, trans. Alan Sheridan (New York: Vintage Books, 1977), 200. Jeremy Bentham, an English philosopher, first described the Panopticon in his work, *Panopticon Letters* (1787).
3. Foucault, *Discipline and Punish: The Birth of the Prison*, 200.
4. Foucault, *Discipline and Punish: The Birth of the Prison*, 201.
5. Foucault, *Discipline and Punish: The Birth of the Prison*, 202.
6. Antonin Artaud, *The Theater and Its Double*, trans. Mary Caroline Richards (New York: Grove Press, Inc., 1958), 30.
7. Foucault, *Discipline and Punish: The Birth of the Prison*, 197.
8. Diderot, Denis, "De la poésie dramatique," in *Oeuvres Esthétiques de Diderot*, ed. Paul Vernière (Paris: Editions Garnier Frères, 1965), 231. Translated from the original French version by the author.
9. Foucault, *Discipline and Punish: The Birth of the Prison*, 206.
10. Gilles Deleuze, *The Fold: Leibniz and the Baroque*, trans. Tom Conley (Minneapolis: University of Minnesota Press, 1993).
11. Peter Eisenman, "Folding in Time: The Singularity of Rebstock," in *D: Columbia Documents of Architecture and Theory, Volume Two* (New York: Columbia University Graduate School of Architecture, Planning and Preservation, 1993) 106.
12. Eisenman, "Folding in Time: The Singularity of Rebstock," 105.
13. Eisenman, "Folding in Time: The Singularity of Rebstock," 104.
14. Richard Riddell, "The German *Raum*," *The Drama Review* 24, no. 1 (March 1980): 39–52.
15. Before this, Minks had explored space and pop art in Zadek's production of a Schiller play *The Robbins*. As a backdrop for a black floor, he had enlarged a Roy Lichtenstein painting of a face with a firing gun, multiple lips, and the word "CRAK!". See Riddell, "The German *Raum*," 40.
16. Luc Bondy and Jurgen Flinm, *Erich Wonder: Stage Design*, ed. Koschk Hetzer-Molden (Ostfidern, Germany: Hatje Cantz Publishers, 2001).
17. Bondy and Flinm, *Eric Wonder: Stage Design*, 46.
18. Heiner Müller, in discussion with the author, May 1991.
19. The major drawback, of course, is a financial one: To actualize any one of the discussed *Raums* one must have a tremendous amount of high-quality technology, and therefore a very high budget.
20. For the 1991 Experimental Theater Ensemble production of *Hamletmachine*, we tried to create a *Raum*, using a room that was carpeted and painted brown. This immediately posed a challenge: the room was brown and carpeted, had windows, and

images could not be well defined using the lights at our disposal. This conflict was a creative challenge, and so we tackled it in creating our *Raum* for the production.

21. Roland Barthes, "Diderot, Brecht, Eisenstein," in *Responsibility of Forms*, trans. by Richard Howard (New York: Farrar, Straus and Giroux, 1985), 89–97.

22. I use the word "image" here instead of "*tableau*" because *tableau*, as we shall see, implies a framed image.

23. Peter Brook, *The Empty Space* (New York: Atheneum, 1968), 9.

24. Barthes, "Diderot, Brecht, Eisenstein," 89.

25. Barthes, "Diderot, Brecht, Eisenstein," 89–90.

26. Barthes, "Diderot, Brecht, Eisenstein," 90.

27. An argument can be made that "environmental theater" is borderless, and that it takes place in an open space with an open-ended stage. Even in this case, the argument for the frame can be extended by the very fact that the open-ended space of this stage is finally and ultimately limited by the eyes. Within an open space, the human eye will create its own borderlines and will impose its own *cadre* onto the representation. Though it may be true that the border and *cadre* of the representation may vary from place to place, depending on where the spectator is seated, each seat of each spectator will create its own frame. In this manner, even the open-ended "environmental theater" will have an audience-imposed frame.

28. Immanuel Kant, *The Critique of Judgment*, trans. James Creed Meredith (Oxford: Clarendon Press, 1952).

29. Jacques Derrida, *The Truth in Painting*, trans. Geoff Bennington and Ian McLeod (Chicago: University of Chicago Press, 1987), 59–60.

30. Derrida, *The Truth in Painting*, 63.

31. Anthony Cooper, Earl of Shaftesbury, *Second Characters*, ed. Benjamin Rand, (Cambridge: Cambridge University Press, 1914), 30–32.

32. Anthony Cooper, Earl of Shaftesbury, *Second Characters*, 30–32.

33. *Merriam-Webster's Collegiate Dictionary,* 10th ed., s.v. "border," "tableau," and "frame."

34. Barthes, "Diderot, Brecht, Eisenstein," 90.

35. Barthes, "Diderot, Brecht, Eisenstein," 90–91.

36. Denis Diderot, "Entretiens sur le Fils Naturel," in *Oeuvres Esthétiques de Diderot*, ed. Paul Vernière (Paris: Editions Garnier Frères, 1965), 88. Translated from the original French by the author.

37. Diderot, "Entretiens sur le Fils Naturel," 139.

38. Michael Fried, *Absorption and Theatricality* (Chicago: University of Chicago Press, 1980), 78.

39. Denis Diderot, "Pensées détachées sur la peinture, la sculpture et la poésie," in *Oeuvres Esthétiques de Diderot*, ed. Paul Vernière (Paris: Editions Garnier Frères, 1965), 780. Translated from the original French version by the author.

40. Diderot's theoretical notions of tableaux and composition have now become essential laws of directing. Of course, there are no formal laws of composition and aesthetics beyond a few elementary principles and common sense. As Liviu Ciulei points out, "There is only one law in the theater: green does not go with red unless it does." In short, use common sense, and do what needs to be done to achieve the aesthetic results for which you aim. As for logic, it is also rooted in common sense and elementary principles. In my first encounter with Ciulei, during his rehearsal of Goldoni's *Squabbles in Chiogga* at New York University, he gently remarked, "Do you know how I work? Logic." The laws of logic and composition do not exclude one another. Nor do they exclude other choices; there is more than one

logical and aesthetically correct choice for a given problem.

41. Bertolt Brecht, "A Short Organum for the Theatre," in *Brecht on Theatre*, ed. and trans. John Willett (New York: Hill and Wang, 1964), 180.

42. Fried, *Absorption and Theatricality*, 92.

43. Roland Barthes, *Camera Lucida: Reflections on Photography*, trans. Richard Howard (New York: Hill and Wang, 1981), 26–27.

44. Diderot, "De la poésie dramatique," 276.

45. Denis Diderot, "Lettres sur les sourds et muets," critical edition by Paul Hugo Meyer in *Diderot Studies VII*, ed. Otis Fellows (Geneva: Librarie Droz, 1965), 47–48.

46. Barthes, "Diderot, Brecht, Eisenstein," 93.

47. Barthes, "Diderot, Brecht, Eisenstein," 93.

48. Carl Weber, "Brecht's Concept of *Gestus* and the American Performance Tradition," in *Brecht Sourcebook*, ed. Carol Martin and Henry Bial (New York: Routledge, 2000), 43.

49. Barthes, "Diderot, Brecht, Eisenstein," 93.

50. Bertolt Brecht, "On Gestic Music," in *Brecht on Theatre*, ed. and trans. John Willett (New York: Hill and Wang, 1964), 104.

51. Bertolt Brecht, "An Interview with an Exile," in *Brecht on Theatre*, ed. and trans. John Willett (New York: Hill and Wang, 1964), 67.

52. Brecht, "A Short Organum for the Theatre," 198.

53. Brecht, "A Short Organum for the Theatre," 204.

54. Brecht, "A Short Organum for the Theatre," 198, 200.

55. Brecht, "A Short Organum for the Theatre," 200.

56. Brecht, "A Short Organum for the Theatre," 201.

57. Bertolt Brecht, "The Modern Theatre Is the Epic Theatre," in *Brecht on Theatre*, ed. and trans. John Willett (New York: Hill and Wang, 1964), 37.

58. Brecht, "A Short Organum for the Theatre," 200.

59. Barthes, "Diderot, Brecht, Eisenstein," 92.

60. Brecht, "A Short Organum for the Theatre," 201.

61. Brecht, "A Short Organum for the Theatre," 201.

62. In this structure, for example, the titles are as follows: I.1 The Noble Child, I.2 The Flight into the Northern Mountains, I.3 In the Northern Mountains; and II.1 The Story of the Judge, II.2 The Chalk Circle.

63. Barthes, "Diderot, Brecht, Eisenstein," 92.

Chapter 3
Sequencing in Time

Cinema resembles so many other arts. If cinema has very literary characteristics, it also has theatrical qualities, a philosophical side, attributes of painting and sculpture and musical elements. But cinema is, in the final analysis, cinema . . . I believe that the essence of the cinema lies in cinematic beauty and that cinematic strength derives from the multiplier effect of sound and visual being brought together.

—Akira Kurosawa[1]

Montage and Narrative

Translated from the French, "montage" means none other than "editing." An immediate and simple way to understand this process is through the editing that takes place in computer word processing. Here, a large part of editing consists of cutting and pasting fragments of texts in different orders and places. This constitutes the simplest level of montage.[2] The second level of montage is defined through a *summation of a series of frames*. This can easily be found in visual fields such as architecture. The noted architect and theoretician John Hejduck[3] describes the architectural process as the culmination of fragments towards a single frame:

> Whatever the initial catalyst is, let us assume that an architect has an architectural image inside his mind's eye. The initial image is like a single still-frame, because I do not believe that at first any architect has a total image of an entire architecture simultaneously. To my experience or knowledge it doesn't work that way. There may be a series of images one after the other over a period of time. But the period of time, no matter how small, is a necessary ingredient for the evolution of totality. It must be understood that "total architecture" is ultimately made up of parts, fragments and fabrications.[4]

The notion of montage is undoubtedly *the* single most important element of filmmaking. Orson Welles highlights it, remarking: "Editing is *the* aspect of cinema." This "editing" is montage. While filmmakers tend to use the term "editing," theoreticians and critics often use the more theoretical term of "montage." Having examined montage in the context of the theater—through the tableau and the structure of theater—let us now examine it more closely from the perspective and the lens of cinema, where the term was originally coined.

The term was first defined and developed by Sergei M. Eisenstein. In "A Dialectic Approach to Film Form," written in Moscow, April 1929, he writes: "Shot and montage are the basic elements of cinema. Montage has been established by the Soviet film as the nerve of cinema."[5] In "The Cinematographic Principle and the Ideogram" (1929) he writes: "Cinematography is, first and foremost, montage."[6] For Eisenstein, montage is the most important cinematic concept, and as we shall see, he defines it in many different fashions.

The seed of the Eisensteinian montage is rooted in theater and theater directing.[7] More specifically, it is rooted in *mise-en-scène* using tableaux. In the first two years of his course on directing at the State Cinema Institute in Moscow, Eisenstein emphasized the study of directing through a thorough study of theater principles. In his essay "Through Theatre to Cinema," written in 1934, he writes:

> The technique of genuine *mise-en-scène* composition was being mastered and approaching its limits. It was already threatened with becoming the knight's move in chess, the shift of purely plastic contours in the already non-theatrical outlines of detailed drawings.
> Sculptural details seen through the frame of the *cadre*, or shot, transitions from shot to shot, appeared to be the logical way out for the threatened hypertrophy of the *mise-en-scène*. Theoretically it established our dependence on *mise-en-scène* and montage. Pedagogically, it determined, for the future, the approaches to montage and cinema, arrived at through the mastering of theatrical construction and through the art of *mise-en-scène*. Thus was born the concept of *mise-en-cadre*. As the *mise-en-scène* is an interrelation of people in action, so the *mise-en-cadre* is the pictorial composition of mutually dependent cadres (shots) in a montage sequence.[8]

The first part of this quote makes a critical observation about the art of directing: Composition and blocking can become so pure, reasonable, and logical that they begin to resemble chess moves or chess "blockings." As for the second half, Eisenstein introduces two key terms to make a distinction in the directing process, and thus montage. They are "cadre" and "shot"—both of which are now common words in the world of cinema and filmmaking.[9]

Eisenstein defines the *shot* as: "A single piece of celluloid. A tiny rectangular frame in which there is, organized in some way, a piece of event."[10] In the language of films, a shot is the picture that is taken on the film; it is the equivalent of the tableau in the theater. (One can even rename the shot as a "film-tableau.") The shot is also defined by the *cadre*, or the "frame" of the shot. The cadre is the frame of representation necessary for the film shot. It is through the frame that the camera views, captures, and represents the shot. The following are the definitions of "shot" and "frame," as given in the *Dictionary of Film Terms*:

SHOT The basic unit of film construction. A shot is the continuous recording of a scene or object from the time the camera starts until it stops. In the edited film it is the length of a film from one splice or optical *transition* to the next.[11]

FRAME Each individual photograph recorded on motion-picture celluloid is referred to as a frame. The frame is the basic visual unit of motion pictures, printed on a strip of celluloid material of varying widths: 8 mm, 16 mm, 35 mm, 65 mm, 70 mm. In sound motion pictures 24 separate frames are photographed and projected per second to create the effect of natural movement on the screen.[12]

It is worth noting that the word "frame," a translation of the French word *cadre*, did not exist in Russian before its introduction into the film vocabulary.[13] The frame is also directly linked to composition and the camera. As Bazin points out in a definition of a frame: "The camera cannot see everything at once but it makes sure not to lose any part of what it chooses to see."[14] This gives montage the authority of precision: "In short, montage by its very nature rules out ambiguity of expression."[15] The notion of film frame also gives rise to "framing," which refers to composition:

FRAMING The act of composing through the viewfinder of the camera the desired view of the images to be photographed. Framing includes choices of camera *angle, angle of view* (scope), and *blocking*. The end result of the photographed scene or shot is also referred to as the *filmmaker's framing*, and is an important consideration in film analysis that examines photographic style.[16]

Eisenstein draws an important distinction between the shot and montage. He writes: "The minimum 'distortable' fragment of nature is the shot; the ingenuity in its combination is montage."[17] This distinction is made constantly throughout his writings. As early as the first page of *Film Form*, he writes: "Without going too far into the theoretical debris of the specifics of cinema, I want here to discuss two of its features. These are features of other arts as well, but the film is particularly accountable to them. *Primo*: photo-fragments of nature are recorded; *secundo*: these fragments are combined in various ways. Thus, the shot (or frame), and thus, montage."[18] The shot is necessary for the creation of montage just as bricks are necessary for the creation of a house. "Cemented together, these shots form montage."[19]

Eisenstein's quote about *mise-en-scène* makes a careful distinction between the external selection (Selection B) and the internal selection (Selection A). For him, rationally enough, the art of composing the frame and the art of shooting the frame—the organizing of the inside works of the frame or cadre—can be redefined and called *mise-en-cadre*, or "that which is placed in the frame." On the other hand, the art of arranging the sequence of frames, of shots, to convey the narrative is called montage, and it belongs to the external selection and the *mise-en-scène*. In this respect, the director has a duel task of: a) composing his frames and shots (Selection A), and b) arranging them in the most suitable and desirable sequence (Selection B). Together, the two tasks create the film, but the latter task—montage—is the more important of the two.

The primary principle of montage lies in *découpage* (cutting) and unity towards a new meaning. In other words, montage is when two different signs are combined to create a new, third meaning. Eisenstein identifies this as the main trait of montage. He writes: "This property reveals that *any two pieces of film stuck together inevitably combine to create a new concept, a new quality born of juxtaposition.*"[20] Indeed, by examining this explanation through the lens of semiotics, we can see that a first sign plus a second sign gives us a third sign, and the third sign has a meaning of its own, independent of the first two.[21] This basic semiotic principle holds true for all "sign systems," and can be applied to any field of language and communication. Eisenstein expands on this point: "This is by no means a specifically cinematographic phenomenon, but one we invariably come across in all cases when two facts, phenomena, or objects are juxtaposed. When we see two objects placed side by side, we draw certain conclusions almost automatically."[22] He illustrates this point with the following example from literature:

> Take, for example, a grave. Imagine a weeping woman in mourning beside it. And it is almost a sure guess that you will conclude that she is *a widow*. The effect of Ambrose Bierce's anecdote "The Inconsolable Widow" (from his Fantastic Fables) is based on this property of our perception. Here is how he told it:
> A woman in widow's weeds was weeping upon a grave.
> "'Console yourself, Madam,' said a Sympathetic Stranger. 'Heaven's mercies are infinite. There is another man somewhere, besides your husband, with whom you can still be happy.' 'There was,' she sobbed, 'there was, but this is his grave.'"[23]

Usually, "a widow + a grave" = "the grave of the husband." In this story, however, the meaning is changed by the third sign, which is independent of the first two: the unexpected "lover."

Eisenstein uses another literary example: "'The raven flew while the dog sat on its tail. Is that possible?'"[24] Again, Eisenstein points out that the standard approach is to add the two signs, as opposed to seeing them independent of one another: "Automatically we take the two elements and add them up. The puzzle is usually put in such a way as to imply that the dog was sitting on the raven's tail while in reality *the two actions* are independent of each other: one, the raven was flying; two, the dog was sitting on *its own* tail."[25] He then proceeds to defend the montage principle: "So there is nothing astonishing in the fact that, given two pieces of film following one after the other, the spectator draws a certain conclusion."[26]

Eisenstein perhaps most clearly illustrates his notion of montage through the Japanese alphabet, which he sees as a language of hieroglyphs and ideograms. In the Japanese language, the combination of two signs gives rise to a third sign—to a third meaning or concept. He cites several examples:

> For example: the picture for water and the picture of an eye signifies 'to weep';
> the picture of an ear near the drawing of a door = 'to listen';
> a dog + a mouth = 'to bark'
> a mouth + a child = 'to scream';
> a mouth + a bird = 'to sing';
> a knife + a heart = 'sorrow,' and so on.
> But this is montage!
> Yes. It is exactly what we do in the cinema, combining shots that are depictive, single in meaning, neutral in content—into intellectual contexts and series.[27]

Juxtaposition is fundamental to the entire montage process. The film we see on screen is created by frames (or shots), one after another, one juxtaposed with the second and third, and so on. In this light, it is practically impossible to speak about the meaning of a single shot on its own. Each frame speaks, but only in conjunction to its previous shot.

In an essay titled "The Filmic Fourth Dimension," Eisenstein emphasizes this chain of signs. He writes:

> The film-frame can never be an inflexible *letter of the alphabet*, but must always remain a multiple-meaning ideogram. And it can be read only in juxtaposition, just as an *ideogram* acquires its specific *significance, meaning*, and even *pronunciation* (occasionally in diametric opposition to one another) only when combined with a separately indicated reading or tiny meaning—an indicator for the exact reading—placed alongside the basic hieroglyph.[28]

A film frame stands on its own with a synchronic meaning, for example, a shot of a "surprised face." Yet in film, the film meaning, which is the third meaning, is only conveyed and completed when the frame is juxtaposed to another frame. Depending on the second frame, the third meaning will vary. Add a gun in the next frame, and the surprised face conveys a scream; add a clown, and the same face can be laughing; add a dead body, and the face is crying, and so on. Eisentein emphasizes, "In my opinion, however, montage is an idea that arises from the collision of independent shots—shots even opposed to one another: the dramatic principle."[29]

Eisenstein's notion of montage is more specifically referred to as "montage of attractions." It is important to note that although Eisenstein was the primary proponent and champion of the montage theory, other directors of the same generation, also contributed to its development and actualization—perhaps not so much in theory, but in practice. In *What Is Cinema?* André Bazin cites and compares the different forms of montage: 1) parallel montage, 2) accelerated montage, and 3) montage by attractions. Parallel montage involves "conveying a sense of simultaneity of two actions taking place at a geographical distance by means of alternating shots from each," while accelerated montage is the illusion of increasing speed. As Bazin explains it, "In *La Roue* Abel Gance created the illusion of the steadily increasing speed of a locomotive without actually using any image of speed (indeed the wheel could have been turning on the spot) simply by a multiplicity of shots of ever decreasing length."[30] Eisenstein's notion of montage, however, is more complex than the others. "Finally there is 'montage by attraction,' the creation of S.M. Eisenstein, and not so easily described as the others, but which may be roughly defined as the reinforcing of the meaning of one image by association with another image not necessarily part of the same episode."[31] Regardless of their different forms, all three, Bazin points out, share the basic definition of montage, "namely, the creation of a sense or meaning not proper to the images themselves but derived exclusively from their juxtaposition."[32]

Inherent in its definition, montage communicates through juxtaposition, and therefore through conflict and clashes. These conflicts and clashes fall within both categories of internal selection/composition (Selection A) and more importantly for cinema and montage, the external selection (Selection B). Each juxtaposition will have two layers of conflict: the first is within the shot—within the composition or internal selection; the second is between the clash of shots—between the frames themselves, or the so-called external selection. Regarding the various levels of conflict, in his essay "A Dialectic Approach to Film Form," Eisenstein lists ten different forms of conflict and demonstrates some with either photos or diagrams, including graphic conflict, conflict of planes, conflict of volumes, spatial conflict, light conflict, and tempo conflict.

The laws of composition, both within the shot as well as with respect to the external sequencing, changes from film to film, depending on the content and genre of the narrative. A "Film Noir" will address one set of aesthetic codes, while a "Thriller" will address another, a "Western" another, and so forth. The composition will also differ from one director to another. There is, however, no doubt about the universality of montage as the primary language of cinema and films. In his essay "Film Language" (1934), Eisenstein defends the art of film together with its young language of montage:

> For many film-makers montage and leftists excesses of formalism—are synonymous. Yet montage is not this at all.
>
> For those who are able, montage is the most powerful compositional means of telling a story.
>
> For those who do not know about composition, montage is a syntax for the

correct construction of each particle of a film fragment.
And lastly, montage is simply an elementary rule of filmography for those who mistakenly put together pieces of a film as one would mix ready-made recipes for medicine, or to pickle cucumbers, or preserve plums, or ferment apples and cranberries together.[33]

At the end of the essay, Eisenstein calls out to other film directors to raise their voices and thoughts in the language of films, in the language of frame/cadre/shot and montage. In the last paragraph of this essay, Eisenstein concludes with an open-ended invitation: "It is time with all sharpness to pose the problem of the culture of film-language. It is important that all film-workers speak out in this cause. And before else, in the language of the montage and shots of their own films."[34]

This invitation was nothing new. It was conceived six years earlier in a joint statement, written on August 5, 1928, by Eisenstein, Pudovkin, and Alexandrov.[35] The call was soon to be repeated, and gradually, it was answered by every filmmaker around the globe. To this day, filmmakers are still responding to Eisenstein's invitation. With every film, from anywhere in the globe, they depend on film's universal language of montage. Montage has become their primary language.

The effect of this language on the world of cinema was such that it created stock formulae and principles for films. Without exception, all directors abided to the standard formula generated by the montage theory: "Thus around 1938 films were edited, almost without exception, according to the same principle. The story was unfolded in a series of set-ups numbering as a rule about 600. The characteristic procedure was by shot-reverse-shot, that is to say, in a dialogue scene, the camera followed the order of the text, alternating the character shown with each speech."[36] Few directors, cinematographers, or editors had any ideas about how to challenge montage theory, until a young theater director, trained against the screen through theater, broke and reformed the cinematic rules. This director was Orson Welles, and the critical film was *Citizen Kane* (1941).[37]

"*Citizen Kane* can never be too highly praised," writes Bazin. "Thanks to the depth of field, whole scenes are covered in one take, the camera remaining motionless. Dramatic effects for which we had formerly relied on montage were created out of the movements of the actors within a fixed framework."[38] The replacement of a scene created through montage with a scene created through the depth of field was a revolution in framing, which reformed montage by injecting the theater into the cinema. Before this new framing device for the cinema, which I refer to as the *[framed theater]*, the theory and practice of montage eliminated the possibility of theatricality on-screen. If it had not been for Welles' usage of the "shot in depth," the creation of the so-called [framed theater]—a sense of the theater within the cinema—might not have been born so early. Bazin makes this observation when he compares Welles' framing with that of other directors:

All you need to do is to compare two frames shot in depth, one from 1910, the other from a film by Wyler or Welles, to understand just by looking at the image, even apart from the context of the film, how different their functions are. The framing in the 1910 film is intended, to all intents and purposes, as a substitute for the missing forth wall of the theatrical stage, or at least in exterior shots, for the best vantage point to view the action, whereas in the second case the setting, the lighting, and the camera angles give an entirely different reading. Between them, director and cameraman have converted the screen into a dramatic checkboard, planned down to the last detail."[39]

Whereas the 1910 "shot in depth" filmed the scene as only a shot among other shots (as if it were nothing else but a mere fourth wall), Welles used the shot in depth to frame, focus, and create the scene as if it were a staged play. The Welles scene is composed down to the last detail—all actions, entrances and exits, and décor are included in the composition *before* its shooting. Bazin continues with a concrete example:

The clearest if not the most original examples of this are to be found in *The Little Foxes* where the *mise-en-scène* takes on the severity of a working drawing. Welles' pictures are more difficult to analyze because of his over-fondness for the baroque. Objects and characters are related in such a fashion that it is impossible for the spectator to miss the significance of the scene. To get the same results by way of montage would have necessitated a detailed succession of shots.[40]

Creating a [framed theater] through his usage of the depth of field, Welles did away with montage; successive shots are no longer a necessity. Instead, a well-composed, well-planned, and well-blocked theater tableau can be framed and shot on film. The camera was at the service of the scene, not vice versa. This revolutionary insight came as a result of Welles' years of experience working with a (static) stage as a theater director. This insight, combined with the courage to apply it to his first film, *Citizen Kane*, created a new method for the cinema. To comprehend and fully appreciate this film, we ought to defer the scrutiny until we have discussed Eisenstein's second theory of montage, namely the notion of "vertical montage."[41] Here, it is sufficient to note that Welles' usage of "shot in depth" to create a [framed theater] was revolutionary. It was not "just a stock in trade of the cameraman," but rather it became a "capital gain in the field of direction—a dialectical step forward in the history of film language."[42]

Application: Montage in Practice

Eisenstein not only gave the world an entire set of films that would become great classics, but he also gave future generations a theory of the "language of film," both practical and abstract. The theory of montage has never been so fully explained and expanded by another filmmaker; this has been the task of critics, philosophers, and film theoreticians. Instead, filmmakers make films and thereby practice the theory, all agreeing with the fact that montage is the primary language of films. In cinema and filmmaking, there is nothing outside of montage. In discussing the making of his first film, *Silver City* (1969), Wim Wenders demarcates the relationship between montage and the film:

> When I was cutting together the ten shots, I realized that after the shot where the man crosses the tracks hell for leather there would be the expectation that every subsequent shot would contain some action. So for the first time I had to consider the order of shots, some kind of dramaturgy. My original idea, simply to run a series of fixed-frame shots, one after the another, "unconnected" and in no special order, became impossible. The assembling of scenes and their arrangement in an order was, it seemed already, a first step towards a narrative. People would see entirely fanciful connections between scenes and interpret them as having narrative intentions. But that is not what I wanted. I was only combining time and space.[43]

"There is nothing outside of montage" seems to be the golden rule in cinema.[44] Yet, it has a prerequisite, one that takes us back to the text and the question of authorship: the script itself. The birth of montage lies in a script, and preferably in one that has been written (or cowritten) by the director himself or herself.[45] Many filmmakers acknowledge the primary principle of the *auteur* theory that the director writing his or her own script is the first step of montage and filmmaking. Martin Scorsese recalls his teacher pointing out early on in his studies: "In fact, when kids would come to him and say, 'I know I can be a great director, I just need a script,' he would tell them they had to write their own scripts if they wanted to direct—no one was going to do it for them."[46] Akira Kurosawa, another great film director, has a similar memory of his mentor, the Japanese film director Yamamoto Kajiro. "Yama-san said: 'If you want to become a film director, first write scripts.' I felt he was right, so I applied myself wholeheartedly to scriptwriting."[47]

A great director can only go so far with a poor script. No matter how well he or she knows montage theory, and how good his or her editing skills are, if the script is a failure, then there is no room for a great film. Towards this end, directors often write their own scripts, or collaborate with a writer to be able to have full control and vision of the film. In his Appendix B to *The Film Form*, an appendix titled "Notes from a Director's Laboratory [During Work on *Ivan the Terrible* (1945)]," Eisenstein talks about the script in the context of a director's vision. He writes:

> The most important thing is to have the vision. The next is to grasp and hold it. In this there is no difference whether you are writing a film-script, pondering the plan of the production as a whole, or thinking out a solution for some par-

ticular detail.

You must see and feel what you are thinking about. You must see and grasp it. You must hold and fix it in your memory and senses. And you must do it at once.[48]

A good idea on its own is not enough; it needs to be visualized and crystallized into a vision. The vision on its own, on the other hand, is also not enough. It needs to become concrete; it must be actualized and implemented. To this end, the work of the director must begin immediately on paper, with pen, ink, and pencils. Federico Fellini, a master of screen images, remarks:

At the beginning of each film I spend the greater part of my time at the desk, and all I do is doodle. It's my method of tracking the film, of beginning to decipher it by means of these scrawls. . . . I don't know where all those doodles came from. I don't mean I don't recognize them. I made them. They are ones I sketched on sheets of large white paper during the preparation of my films. It's a kind of mania I have, always scribbling. . . . Even the driver's license I have in my pocket is filled with designs. But as regards the designs I sketched at the beginning of each film, they are a way of making notes, of fixing ideas.[49]

Eisenstein continues his explanation:

When you are in a good working mood, images swarm through your busy imagination. Keeping up with them and catching them is very much like grappling with a run of herring.

You suddenly see the outline of a whole scene and, rising simultaneously before this inner eye, a close-up in full detail: a head nesting on a great white ruff.

Just as you are seizing from passing figures in your imagination a characteristic bend of Tzar Ivan's back in the confessional, you must drop your pencil and take up your pen to sketch the dialogue for this scene, and before the ink of this is dry, your pencil is once more making a note of an image that came to you during the dialogue—of the priest's long white hair descending like a canopy over the Tzar's graying head. Before this mood has finished, you find yourself drawing with your pen and penciling notes for the dialogue—on the sheets of drawings.[50]

These sheets of drawings also contain details of costumes, props, gestures, and more important, directions: "Directions become drawings; the voices and intonations of various characters are drawn as series of facial expressions. Whole scenes first take shape as batches of drawings before they take on the clothing of words."[51] In this manner, "mountains of folders, stuffed with drawings, accumulate around the writing of the script—these multiply as the production plans are conceived—and they become a storage problem as the details of sequences and *mise-en-scène* are worked out."[52] The same goes for most directors: *mise-en-scène* means *visualizing*. In today's language of *mise-en-scène*, the scripted drawings are called the storyboard.

Almost all film narratives (scripts) are storyboarded by the director, a technique also used heavily by theater directors,[53] which illuminates the story, shot by shot and frame by frame. Ingmar Bergman recalls how, as a young child, he would make films through a storyboard: "In my childhood I used to draw films, and tried to narrate what happened without using dialogue."[54]

The storyboard essentially reveals the entire film, through montage of frames. The frames include the details of the *mise-en-scène*, as well as precise point of view (long shots or close-ups) and the rhythm of the script. A close neighbor of the shooting script is the classic *bande dessinée* (French for "comic strip"). Inherent in its name, *bande dessinée*, lies a definition of montage: "bande" means "strip" or "track." *Bande dessinée* thus means a visual track of drawings—carefully drawn, carefully framed, and carefully selected frames.

The *bande dessinée* is a narrative told through words and drawings using a designed and ordered frame-by-frame approach. It is a tale told through visual montage. The storyboard, in this light, is then nothing but a "montage on paper." The importance of the storyboard should not be underestimated, for it constitutes the first *mise-en-scène*; it is essentially the closest work of art to the cinema. If each frame were to be filmed separately and pasted together, the final product would be a cartoon film.

Discussing *Taxi Driver* (1975), which won the Cannes Palme d'Or, Martin Scorsese explains, "Because of the low budget, the whole film was drawn out on storyboards, even down to medium close-ups of people talking, so that everything would connect. I had to create this dream-like quality in those drawings. Sometimes the character himself is on the dolly, so that we look over his shoulder as he moves towards another character, and for a split second the audience would wonder what was happening."[55] Figure 3.1 shows a portion of this storyboard—a montage on paper.

Beyond the storyboard lies the actual montage on film. A film begins with a script, then moves into a shooting script, and is then finalized into a film during the third and the last step: shooting and montage. Many film directors agree upon the centrality of this final step of montage. François Truffaut sees the montage as the third form of *mise-en-scène*: "The shooting script [which includes the storyboard] obviously doesn't constitute a literary work but is already a first *mise-en-scène*. The direction [framing and shooting] comprises a second *mise-en-scène*, the editing [montage] a third."[56] "For me," Orson Welles remarks in 1962, the year of *The Trial*, "editing isn't an aspect of cinema, it is *the* aspect."[57] This statement, coming from a director who created the world's "greatest film" by defying the laws of montage twenty-one years earlier, is almost a repentance.

According to some directors, montage gives life to cinema. For Kurosawa, montage is what brings the film to life: "When I reached a certain level of achievement in scriptwriting, Yama-san told me to start editing. I already knew

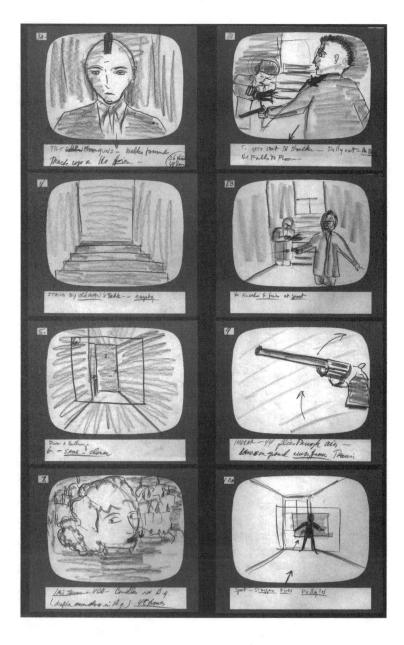

Figure 3.1. Storyboard for *Taxi Driver*, Martin Scorsese, 1975. Courtesy of the Martin Scorsese Collection.

that you can't be a film director if you can't edit. Film editing involves putting on the finishing touches. More than this, it is a process of breathing life into the work."[58] Fellini affirms this vital point, using a somewhat odd metaphor: "It is like when Dr. Frankenstein, his monster constructed of diverse anatomical parts, makes the stretcher rise up to the storm-filled sky to receive life from the thunderous discharge of the lightning. It is with montage that the film begins to breathe, to move, to look you in the eye."[59]

As in writing, editing is the single most important tool for clarity in the communication of the filmmaker's thoughts and vision. It is here that the final story the audience sees takes shape. The difficulty of montage involves objectivity. The writer-director must have the strength to look at the work objectively, "cut" what is not necessary, and keep the essential elements. Bergman locates the frenzy during the shooting process, and objectifies the editing process: "When I see the takes in the cutting room my attitude to the material is completely matter of fact. It's *before* it has taken shape, *before* the camera has absorbed it, that the great frenzy rages."[60] In the same light, Fellini emphasizes privacy and concentration required for the montage: "During the actual shooting I don't at all mind visits from friends, acquaintances or, as is now the custom, entire classes of students noisily entering the theater. (Their comments don't bother me and I even feel stimulated playing at mountebank or juggler.) However, in the little montage studio I tolerate no presence, except of course the editor and his assistants. I must be alone. This is the phase in which the film begins to reveal itself for what it is."[61] On the role of objectivity in montage, Kurosawa remarks:

> The most important requirement for editing is objectivity. No matter how much difficulty you had in obtaining a particular shot, the audience will never know. It is not interesting, it simply isn't interesting. You may have been full of enthusiasm during the filming of a particular shot, but if that enthusiasm doesn't show on screen, you must be objective enough to cut it.[62]

Elsewhere, he remarks:

> But, no matter how much work the director, the assistant director, the cameraman or the lighting technicians put into a film, the audience never knows. What is necessary is to show them something that is complete and has no excess. When you are shooting, of course, you film only what you believe is necessary. But very often you realize only after having shot it that you didn't need it after all. You don't need what you don't need. Yet human nature wants to place value on things in direct proportion to the amount of labor that went into making them. In film editing, this natural inclination is the most dangerous attitude. The art of cinema has been called an art of time, but time used to no purpose cannot be called anything but wasted time.[63]

Montage also means sequencing in time. In this light, Wim Wenders defines films as "congruent time-sequences." He writes: "Films are congruent time-sequences, not congruent ideas. . . . The continuity of movement and action must be true, there mustn't be any jolt in time being portrayed. . . . It doesn't matter what kind of film it is, I just think it should keep faith with the passage in time."[64] Actions in time will yield different stories and different narratives. The story aside, the script written, montage decides on rhythm and tempo and how the story needs to be seen or presented. It is here in the editing room that the director finally "writes" the film. His or her montage determines the final story in every aspect, including the mood, pace, and rhythm. To illustrate the importance of montage in determining the story in its final form, consider the following account from Kurosawa's experience as an assistant director:

> But there is one more incident involving editing and Yama-san that I would like to relate. It took place during the editing of the film Uma (Horses), which I had co-scripted and which Yama-san had put entirely in my hands for cutting. There is one place in the story where a foal has been sold and the mare frantically searches for her baby. Completely crazed, she kicks down her stable door and tries to crawl under the paddock fence. I edited the sequence most diligently to show her expressions and actions in a dramatic way.
>
> But when the edited scene was run through a projector, the feeling didn't come through at all. The mother horse's sorrow and panic somehow stayed flat behind the screen. Yama-san had sat with me and watched the film as I was editing it any number of times, but he never said a word. If he didn't say, "That's good," I knew it meant it was no good. I was at an impasse, and in my despair I finally begged his advice. He said, "Kurosawa, this sequence isn't drama. It's mono-no-aware." Mono-no-aware, "sadness at the fleeting nature of things," like the sweet, nostalgic sorrow of watching the cherry blossoms fall—when I heard this ancient poetic term, I was suddenly struck by enlightenment as if waking from a dream. "I understand!" I exclaimed and set about completely re-editing the scene.
>
> I put together long shots. It became a series of glimpses of a tiny silhouette of the galloping mare, her mane and tail flying in the wind on a moonlight night. And that alone proved sufficient. Even without putting in any sound, it seemed to make you hear the pathetic whinnying of the mother horse and a mournful melody of woodwinds.[65]

A skilled director, then, is one who has developed perfection with respect to montage. An artful montage is one in which the knots between the frames are completely invisible to the eye. Between each cut, there is a small metaphorical space—an incision, a gap—that needs to be covered up through an understanding of time and thus a correct selection of frames. A "rough cut" does not hide the knots, but shows the jumps.[66] Again, to demonstrate the invisibility of montage, Kurosawa recalls the work of another of his mentors:

> Naruse's method consists of building one very brief shot on top of another, but when you look at them all spliced together in the final film, they give the im-

pression of a single long take. The flow is so magnificent that the splices are invisible. This flow of short shots that looks calm and ordinary at first glance then reveals itself to be like a deep river with a quiet surface disguising a fast-raging current underneath. The sureness of his hand in this was without comparison.[67]

Sometimes, to achieve a smooth effect, a scene needs to be shot in a series of takes, and then edited and complied. Other times, a scene benefits from a static camera and a single shot that can communicate and translate the scene to the audience in a single frame. As Wenders points out: "The choice between having a mobile or a fixed camera is a fundamental stylistic one. The term 'fixed camera' sounds so restrictive. It can be quite exhilarating."[68]

Since montage is a sequencing of selected frames, the choice of each shot becomes an important part of the montage process. Montage cannot work miracles; a good montage with horrid frames cannot result in a decent film. To maintain absolute control of the frame, Fellini chose to use the fixed camera to accentuate space as well as to achieve precision in framing. "As far as my films are concerned, I move the camera very little. As I believe in expression, what matters is the way the space is cut up, the precision of what happens within the magical space of the frame, where I refuse to allow the smallest clumsiness. I become furious if there is a wrong movement, or a bad patch of lighting."[69] Bergman's highly psychological films often use the fixed camera. The fixed camera can pull the spectator right into the heart of the scene, avoiding all possible extra-motions that montage can induce:

> The more excited, the more raw, horrible, brutal, or elaborate a scene is, the better it is to keep the camera an objective median. If the camera gets all excited and begins skipping about all over the bloody place, you lose a lot. It's you, the "audience", who must feel it, whom it's got to strike. If the camera forces its way between and begins talking about its own emotions, usually it will get in the way, and prevent you from experiencing anything. The story mustn't only have a suggestive effect on Elizabeth, it must have a suggestive effect on you, enable you to experience it all down inside you, in your own cinematograph much more drastically, brutally, honestly, and voluptuously than I could ever show.[70]

Beyond the static camera, montage can take place during shooting. As with Kurosawa, Bergman had a mentor to teach him the art of montage. Recalling his early years as a director, Bergman expresses his debt to his film editor, Oscar Rosander, whom Bergman remembers "actually looked like a pair of scissors." Rosander pointed out that montage could take place not only in the editing room, but also behind the camera. While the editor "cuts" in the editing room, the director can often save a great deal of trouble by shouting "cut" during a shooting. Bergman recalls: "He also initiated me into the secrets of editing, among other things a fundamental truth—that editing occurs during filming itself, the rhythm created in the script. I know that many directors hold the opposite view. For me, Oscar Rosander's teaching has been fundamental."[71]

Oscar Rosander's lesson has now become a permanent part of Bergman's vocabulary. He now uses this technique in order to write scripts: "Nowadays I don't write dialogue at all, only a suggestion of what it could be. The script is nothing else but a collection of motifs that I work over with my actors as the filming proceeds. The final decisions I make in the cutting room, where I cut away all obtrusive elements."[72]

Bergman also uses this lesson to shape the script and give the film its rhythm. "I've always made a sport of cutting with the camera. There's a special sensuous delight in scrubbing as few feet of film as possible, in knowing exactly where a scene is to change. In this way a film acquires its rhythm, even while it's being shot. Your actors get the feel of the rhythms you intend, and work with even greater insight as the film proceeds."[73] Bergman notes another advantage of montage during the shoot: It can not only determine the rhythm of the scenes, but it can also determine the film's overall fluidity and illusionary quality, a very important aspect for the *mise-en-scène* that few directors ever obtain.

> The rhythm in my films is conceived in the script, at the desk, and is then given birth in front of the camera. All forms of improvisation are alien to me. If I am ever forced into hasty decisions, I grow sweaty and rigid with terror. Filming for me is an illusion planned in detail, the reflection of a reality which the longer I live seems to me more and more illusionary.
>
> When film is not a document, it is a dream. That is why Tarkovsky is the greatest of them all. He moves with such naturalness in the room of dreams. He doesn't explain. What should he explain anyhow? He is a spectator, capable of staging his visions in the most unwieldy but, in a way, the most willing of media. All my life I have hammered on the doors of the rooms in which he moves so naturally. Only a few times have I managed to creep inside. Most of my conscious efforts have ended in embarrassing failures—*The Serpent's Egg, The Touch, Face to Face* and so on.
>
> Fellini, Kurosawa and Bunuel move in the same fields as Tarkovsky.[74]

The directors that Bergman cites are among the greatest directors of film history. Each is a filmmaker who writes and directs his own script. Thus, montage is only another pen for their final writing of the film. The director who works on his or her own scripts and montage ultimately determines the structure of his or her films. For example, for Kurosawa, the best structure of a film is either a) that of a symphony with three or four movements, all differing in tempo, or b) that of the Noh play structure with its three parts: *jo* (introduction), *ha* (destruction), and *kyù* (haste). Ultimately, Kurosawa remarks, "I think the symphonic structure is the easiest for people of today to understand."[75]

In developing his film *The Silence* (1962), Bergman remembers the origin of the film was in a piece of music in Bartók's *Concerto for Orchestra*. The film began with this piece, and was structured after it, but, in the end, only a small portion of it was left incorporated:

My original idea was to make a film that should obey musical laws, instead of dramaturgical ones. A film acting by association—rhythmically, with themes and counter-themes. As I was putting it together, I thought much more in musical terms than I'd done before. All that is left of Bartók is the very beginning. It follows Bartók's music rather closely—the dull continuous note, then the sudden explosion.[76]

During a collaborative session between Herbert von Karajan and Ingmar Bergman on the opera *Turandot*, Karajan remarks to Bergman, "I saw your production of *Dream Play*. You direct as if you were a musician. You've a feeling for rhythm, the musicality, pitch."[77] Karajan's observations are rather accurate because a director needs to be a conductor, both on stage and on screen, holding on to all the elements pertinent to audio and visual composition. Karajan continues, now criticizing Bergman's montage for its lack of respect and tact in filming Mozart's *Magic Flute*: "That was in your *Magic Flute* too. In parts it was charming, but I didn't like it. You'd switched some scenes at the end. You can't do that with Mozart. Everything is organic."[78]

Indeed, Karajan may be right about Mozart and his music, but when it comes to film and directing, Bergman is the director and it is his prerogative to rearrange through montage. If, in cinema, the director is the equivalent of the conductor of an orchestra, then montage is his baton. And this baton must conduct the details and the rhythm of the composition—both visual as well as audio.

The visual combined with the audio is what gives the screen its final composition—its final cinematographic quality. On numerous occasions, Kurosawa defines the cinematic beauty as the unity between the sound and the image. For him, cinema is unique, especially in its unity of sound and visuals: "But cinema is, in the final analysis, cinema. . . . I believe that the essence of the cinema lies in cinematic beauty."[79] Kurosawa explains his notion of cinematic beauty as follows: "My pet theory—that cinematic strength derives from the multiplier effect of sound and visual being brought together—was born from the experience of Yama-san's dubbing work."[80] The "dubbing" of sound with images is also a form of montage, known as "vertical montage."

Vertical Montage: The Invisible Link

In his essay "A Dialectic Approach to Film Form," Eisenstein begins with a quote from Goethe's "Conversations with Eckermann" (5 June 1825): "In nature we never see anything isolated, but everything in connection with something else which is before it, beside it, under it, and over it."[81] Later, in another essay titled "A Course in Treatment," Eisenstein writes the following about cinematography and the frame:

It is true that in practice a film is broken up into separate episodes. But these episodes all hang from the rod of a single ideological, compositional and stylistic whole.

The art of cinematography is not in selecting a fanciful framing, or in taking something from a surprising camera angle.

The art is in every fragment of a film being an organic part of an organically conceived whole.[82]

An essential element of every frame, as well as the film as an organic whole, is the element of sound—the audio track or the "soundtrack." The two sensations, though different in their nature (of perception)—"I see" vs. "I hear"—when combined yield the single unit of perception of "I feel." It is on this basis, the combination of sound and image, that Eisenstein wanted to define the future of cinema. In "The Filmic Fourth Dimension" (1929), he writes:

And yet we *cannot reduce aural* and *visual* perceptions to a common denominator. They are values of different dimensions. But the visual overtone and the sound overtone are values of a *singly measured* substance. Because, if the frame is a *visual perception,* and the tone is an aural perception, *visual as well as aural overtones are a totally physiological sensation.* And, consequently, they are *of one and the same kind,* outside the sound or aural categories that serve as guides, conductors to its achievement.

For the musical overtone (a throb) it is not strictly fitting to say: "I hear."

Nor for the visual overtone: "I see."

For both, a new uniform formula must enter our vocabulary: "I feel."[83]

Eisenstein concludes with: "And from the contrapuntal conflict between the visual and the *aural overtones* will be born the composition of the Soviet sound film."[84] The birth of the Soviet sound film to which Eisenstein is referring to is, in essence, the birth of contemporary cinema as we know it today. It was not until the advent of "vertical montage" that the full definition of cinema emerged.

In his last essay in *Film Form,* "Dickens, Griffith, and the Film Today," written in 1944, Eisenstein refers to the audiovisual, or *vertical,* montage: "Montage removes its last contradictions by abolishing duelist contradictions and mechanical parallelism between the realms of sound and sight in what we understand as audiovisual (vertical) montage."[85] Through the vertical montage, the audio and the visual tracks are united to yield the single audiovisual tracked film we know today.

In his first book, *The Film Sense,* written in 1942, Eisenstein fully spells out his theory of vertical montage. In the essay titled "Synchronization of Senses," he writes:

Representation A and *representation B* must be so selected from all the possible features within the theme that is being developed, must be so sought for, that their *juxtaposition*—the juxtaposition of *those very elements* and not of alternative ones—shall evoke in the perception and feelings of the spectator the most complete *image of the theme itself*.[86]

The final work of art, therefore, should use all the senses in a unified manner, to communicate and evoke feelings and thoughts from its viewers. In writing about Leonardo da Vinci's *The Deluge*, for example, Eisenstein points out how all the various elements combine and function as a whole: ". . . those that are purely plastic (the visual element), those indicating human behavior (the dramatic element), and the noise of the crashing and crying (the sound element)—all equally fuse into a single, unifying definitive image of a deluge."[87] All the senses join forces to complete the final image, the final work of art.

Keeping this fact in mind, Eisenstein points out that, in principle, nothing changes in the shift from silent montage to sound-picture montage: ". . . the conception of montage that has been presented here encompasses equally the montage of the silent film and of the sound film."[88] However, a different technical approach is necessary. While working on *Alexander Nevsky* (1938), Eisenstein coined a term for this: *vertical montage*.[89]

Eisenstein borrowed this term from the orchestra score, which is a vertical score that ranges from time zero to time x in a horizontal manner—much like the movement of a film strip. Yet, between the sections of the notes, there are several vertical staffs that function on two levels. On one level, they group the similar instruments together, and on a second level they interrelate all the elements of the orchestra within each unit of time. In this manner, "through the progression of the vertical line, pervading the entire orchestra, and interwoven horizontally, the intricate harmonic musical movement of the whole orchestra moves forward."[90]

The basic principle governing vertical montage the super-imposition of the audiotrack onto the visual track. Through vertical montage, the film becomes a double-tracked entity. Eisenstein explains, "In order to diagram what takes place in vertical montage, we may visualize it as two lines, keeping in mind that each of these lines represents a whole complex of a many-voiced scoring. The search for correspondence must proceed from the intention of matching both picture and music to the general, complex 'imagery' produced by the whole."[91] Figure 3.2 illustrates Eisenstein's own illustration of the one-to-one super-imposition of the two tracks.

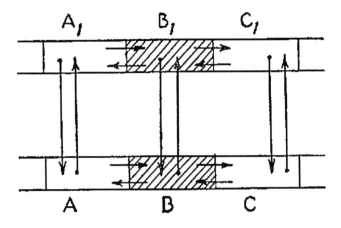

Figure 3.2. "Diagram 2," illustrating vertical montage, *The Film Sense*, Sergei
Eisenstein, 1942. Reprinted with permission from Harcourt Brace & Company.

He explains:

> Diagram 2 reveals the new "vertical" factor of intercorrespondance, which
> arises the moment that the pieces of the sound-picture montage are connected.
> From the viewpoint of montage structure, we no longer have a simple
> horizontal succession of pictures, but now a new "super-structure" is erected
> vertically over the horizontal picture structure. Piece for piece these new strips
> in the "super-structure" differ in length from those in the picture structure, but,
> needless to say, they are equal in total length. Pieces of sound do not fit into the
> picture pieces in sequential order, but in simultaneous order.[92]

As an example of how this vertical montage works in practice, Eisenstein
writes:

> It was exactly this kind of "welding," further complicated (or perhaps further
> simplified?) by another line—the sound-track—that we tried to achieve in *Al-
> exander Nevsky*, especially in the sequence of the attacking German knights
> advancing across the ice. Here the lines of the *sky's tonality—clouded or clear*,
> of the accelerated *pace* of the riders, of their *direction*, of *the cutting back and
> forth* from Russians to knights, of the faces in close-up and the *total* long-shots,
> the *tonal* structure of the music, its *themes*, its *tempi*, its *rhythm*, etc.—created a
> task no less difficult than that of the silent sequence above. Many hours went
> into fusing of these elements into an *organic* whole.[93]

Vertical montage was considerably more difficult before the advent of
sound synchronicity, which did not emerge until 1929. Thus, Eisenstein had to

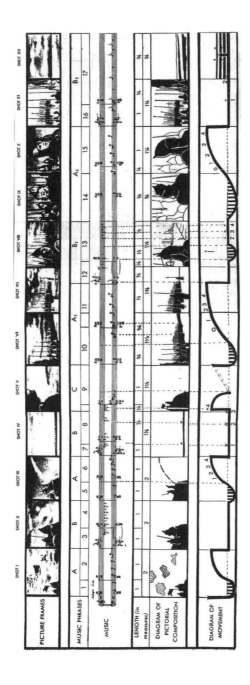

Figure 3.3. A section of the vertical montage, *Alexander Nevsky*, Segei Eisenstein, 1938. Reprinted with permission from Harcourt Brace & Company.

compose the relationship between sound and image in each frame of his sequences. Consider, for example, the following direction he gives to the composer:

> A composer must proceed in the same way when he takes up a previously cut
> film sequence: he is obliged to analyze the visual movement both through its
> overall montage construction and the compositional line carried from indi-
> vidual shot-to-shot even the composition within the shots. He will have to
> base his musical imagery composition on these elements.[94]

Though the final correlation between sight and sound is harmonious on
screen, the actual composition and planning is not always clear to the eyes of the
non-director. For example, Figure 3.3 provides a portion of Eisenstein's audiovisual montage analysis from *Alexander Nevsky*. Martin Scorsese recalls the first
few times he saw the film: "Seeing the design of the film, I fell under the spell
of Eisenstein and his style of editing."[95] In this case, Scorsese is referring to the
totality of the montage—the *montage of attractions* and the *vertical montage*.

If today many directors use music as a significant part of their *mise-en-
scène* vocabulary, it is thanks to the advent of this most crucial concept. Vertical
montage encompasses all that is part of the world of sound—music, speech, and
all types of sound effects. The following section highlights the importance of
this notion through several examples of how filmmakers have applied it on-
screen.

Application: Vertical Montage in Filmmaking

One of the most striking illustrations of the significance of vertical montage is
Walt Disney's *Fantasia* (1940). This film is a vertical montage of a an animated
bande dessinée and classical music. In this film, Walt Disney has animated several selected pieces of classical music, such as Bach's *Toccata* and *fugue in C
minor* and Tchaikovsky's *Shchelkunchik* (*Nutcracker*) *Suite*. The result is an
extraordinary blend of music and visuals, and one must admire the craftmanship
behind it. However, Heiner Müller pointed out the possible negative effects of
vertical montage:

> Fantasia. A musical. I don't need to tell you what it is about. What was so bar-
> baric about this film, something I learned later, was that every American school
> child between the ages of six and eight gets to view it. Which means that for
> the rest of their lives these children will never again be able to hear certain mu-
> sic without seeing those Disney figures and images. The horrifying thing for
> me in this is the occupation of the imagination by clichés which will never go
> away. The use of images to prevent experiences, to prevent the having of expe-
> riences.[96]

Film—an audiovisual art—is also closely related to memory and recollection. As Wim Wenders put it, "Every film starts off from memories, and every film is also a sum of many memories. Then again, every film creates memories. The cinema itself has created many memories."[97] In effect, what we see on screen is something we will retain in our minds; what we sing or hum in the shower will be a trace of a film score; and what we experience audiovisually as children we may retain in our adulthood.

For the director, this personal memory can often be a primary source for the soundtrack. Scorsese notes that his film *Mean Streets* (1973) "featured the music that I grew up with and that music would give me images. . . But for me *Mean Streets* had the best music because it was what I enjoyed and it was part of the way we lived. Suddenly a piece would come on and we'd stay with it for two or three minutes. Life would stop, so I wanted the film to stop and go with the music. *Mean Streets* has that quality, whether it's rock 'n' roll, opera, or Neapolitan love songs."[98] In his account of writing and directing *Rashomon* (1950), Kurosawa explains the role of memory and his vertical montage:

> As I was writing the script, I heard the rhythms of a bolero in my head over the episode of the woman's side of the story. I asked Hayasaka to write a bolero kind of music for the scene. When we came to the dubbing of the scene, Hayasaka sat down next to me and said, "I'll try it with the music." In his face I saw uneasiness and anticipation. My own nervousness and expectancy gave me a painful sensation in my chest. The screen lit up with the beginning of the scene, and the strains of the bolero music softly counted out the rhythm. As the scene progressed, the music rose, but the image and the sound failed to coincide and seemed to be at odds with each another. "Damn it," I thought. The multiplication of sound and image that I had calculated in my head had failed, it seemed. It was enough to make me break out in a cold sweat.[99]

However, rather than stopping the film, rewinding, and recomposing, the composer and Kurosawa adhered to Eisenstein's rule of montage, and let the film roll on, to see it in its entirety. This action, taken in good faith, led to a powerful result:

> We kept going. The bolero music rose yet again, and suddenly picture and sound fell into perfect unison. The mood created was positively eerie. I felt an icy chill run down my spine, and unwittingly I turned to Hayasaka. He was looking at me. His face was pale, and I saw that he was shuddering with the same eerie emotion I felt. From that point on, sound and image proceeded with incredible speed to surpass even the calculations I had made in my head. The effect was strange and overwhelming.[100]

The use of memory to choose a piece of music, and the audiovisual montage to create art, is a personal matter. And yet, vertical montage has become an invisible part not only of the private, but also of the public sphere. How many times do we hear a classical tune, and the other person standing there links it with a television advertisement: "Isn't that the tune for 'such-and-such'?" they ask. Vertical montage has more significantly become a regular and permanent experience for young people: the twenty-four-hour MTV. Scorsese remarks: "One of the things I have against rock videos is that they specify certain images in your mind for each song. I would rather make up my own imagery for the music."[101]

Although the basic elements of vertical montage are common to all, each director has a different sense of music, relationship to sound, and therefore a different style of vertical montage. Almost always, the specific use of vertical montage becomes a visible and essential signature of the director. If the critic cannot recognize the director from his or her employment of the visual montage, he or she can most probably reveal the director's signature through a close scrutiny of the use of vertical montage. While some directors—such as Stanley Kubrick, director of *2001: A Space Odyssey* (1968) and *Clockwork Orange* (1971), or David Lynch, director of the highly acclaimed experimental film *Eraserhead* (1977) and the 1990 Cannes Palme d'Or winner *Wild at Heart*—place a significant accent on the music and soundtrack, others, such as Bergman or Kurosawa, use vertical montage simply to have the text heard or to create a subtle hum in the background, reenforcing the visual theme of the tableau.

For Federico Fellini, vertical montage is a fundamental element of filmmaking. It is where all the script, the dialogue, and the sound is written and added. "For me," admits Fellini, "dubbing [vertical montage] is one of the most demanding phases. I have to rewrite all the dialogue completely, because my way of making a film prohibits my using even one meter of the original soundtrack."[102] He continues to explain the reason for the prohibition. The original soundtrack is "a Tower of Babel: voices of every nationality, dialects, prayers, voices which recite numbers instead of giving cues, voices which at my suggestion tell what they had eaten the night before."[103] He concludes by stating, "Dubbing is like remaking the film, this time according to the needs of the soundtrack, which sometimes presents verbal problems as important as the visual ones."[104]

For Fellini, the role of the vertical montage is particularly important as a result of two technical choices. First, all his films (including his early ones) are post-synched, meaning that the sound is added to the image after the film has been made, because "the noises one can get in the sound studio are very much better—quite apart from trick and artifice—than those one can get by recording the sound live during filming. . . . It is the Americans who insist on recording the sound during filming."[105] This is equally true of the dialogue: "I put dialogue into the film after I have made it. The actor plays better that way, not having to remember his lines. This is all the more so because I often use non-actors and, in order to make them behave naturally, I get them to talk as they would in real life."[106] The second reason is related to Fellini's usage and under-emphasis on dialogue. For Fellini, dialogue is not as central as the other elements of a film. "Dialogue is not important to me. The function of dialogue is merely to inform. I think that in the cinema it is much better to use other elements, such as lighting, objects, and the setting in which the action takes place, since these are more expressive than pages and pages of dialogue. The sound effects should aim to emphasize the image. I work on the sound-track myself, after making the film."[107]

Differences in style are not just limited to how the vertical montage takes place. Choices about what type of music should go with which scenes are equally critical. For example, you can use a "jolly" piece of music with a sad scene (counterpoint), a sad piece of music for a sad scene (accompaniment), or no music at all—simply sounds, silence, or text. As Kurosawa describes it:

> I changed my thinking about musical accompaniment from the time Hayasaka Fumio began working with me as composer of my film scores. Up until that time film music was nothing more than accompaniment—for a sad scene there was always sad music. This is the way most people use music, and it is ineffective. But from *Drunken Angel* onward, I have used light music for some key sad scenes, and my way of using music has differed from the norm—I don't put it in where most people do. Working with Hayasaka, I began to think in terms of the counterpoint of sound and image as opposed to the union of sound and image.[108]

In addition to the "union"/"counterpoint" usage of music, music can be used to highlight the action/mood of the scene; or it can be used to highlight a character throughout the film by giving him/her a theme. Recalling *Seven Samurai* (1954), Kurosawa points out the usage of this highlighting: "I use different theme music for each main character or for different groups of characters."[109]

The "union"/"counterpoint" usage of music was an essential ingredient in Stanley Kubrick's film directing—as essential as movement within the visual montage. He used music to stylize violence and sexuality to such a degree that his images become almost a dance. Consider his own description of *Clockwork Orange* (1971), in which he uses the famous Overture to Rossini's *Thieving Magpie*: "In a very broad sense, you can say the violence is turned into dance. From the rape on the stage of the derelict casino, to the super-frenzied fight, through the water's edge, and the encounter with the cat lady where the giant phallus is pitted against the bust of Beethoven, movement, cutting, and music are the principal considerations."[110]

Kubrick's usage of vertical montage—more significantly through music and creation of soundtracks—is unlike any that of any other director. His selections are often classical pieces of music that can act as a narrative backdrop for his imagery and action. Consider *2001: A Space Odyssey*. The film begins with the music of Richard Strauss's *Also Sprach Zarathustra* slowly revealing the dawn of man, symbolized by a grouping of primates, a large monolith, and a bone,

which when thrown, thanks to montage, becomes a spaceship. The visual inter-
connection of a bone with a spaceship is highlighted even further by the usage of
vertical montage. The bone is set to Richard Strauss's *Zarathustra* score, and
while the transformed spaceship floats in the void, in the vast emptiness of
space, to a slow movement of Johann Strauss's waltz, *The Blue Danube*. This
segment of the waltz serves as the spaceship's theme; together *The Blue Danube*
and the slow floating of the spaceship in time and space create an extraordinary
atmosphere of peace, freedom, and eternity. The monolith that appeared in the
beginning of the film appears several times again with its own theme: Gyorgy
Ligeti's *Requiem*.

Apart from the music, sound on its own, as an independent entity, can be
another important feature of films and the vertical montage. Kurosawa remarks:
"Depending on how the sound is put in, the visual image may strike the viewer
in many different ways."[111] He recalls how his mentor, Yama-san, taught him
the superimposition of the vertical montage on the visuals: "Yama-san seemed
to enjoy surprising us, so he took care not to let us know what he was doing.
Then he would gleefully surprise us with an extraordinary combination of sound
effects and music. The sound powerfully altered the visual image to create a
whole new impression, and at these moments we forget all our pain and exhaus-
tion in the excitement of it."[112] Kurosawa observes that sound and music co-
exist with one another: "From the moment I begin directing a film, I am thinking
about not only the music but the sound effects as well. Even before the camera
rolls, along with all the other things I consider, I decide what kind of sound I
want."[113]

The usage and design of sound in films is no easier than that of music. In
fact, due to its fragmentary nature, sounds can rapidly become much more complicated and frustrating. Scorsese recalls his experience with sound on *The
Raging Bull* (1980):

> The sound on *Raging Bull* was particularly difficult because each punch, each
> camera click and each flashbulb was different. The sound effects were done by
> Frank Warner, who had worked on *Close Encounters of the Third Kind* and
> *Taxi Driver*. He used rifle shots and became very possessive and even burnt
> them afterwards so nobody else could use them. The fight scenes were done in
> Dolby stereo, but the dialogue was recorded normally, and that caused us
> something of a problem. We anticipated about eight weeks of mixing and I
> think it took sixteen weeks. It was murder, mainly because each time we had a
> fight scene, it had to have a different aura.[114]

Among the many significant contemporary directors, David Lynch use
vertical montage in a completely unique manner. He places the accent on sound
and micro-sounds. The audiotrack of his first film, *Eraserhead* (1977) is entirely
composed of sounds and sound effects, forming a sort of essay in sound–image
correlation. The score is a recording of industrial sounds—steam, steel, water

metals, elevator sounds, and other machines. Dialogue is included also, though it might as well not have been. The film, striking in its black-and-white photography, uses the vertical track not only to create atmosphere for its images, but also to control them. In his later films, Lynch increases the level of text and music in his soundtrack. In *The Elephant Man* (1980), another black-and-white film, Lynch uses sound to create an atmosphere for the grotesque. It may be hard to imagine how sound could create an atmosphere for a particular image, such as the deformed and grotesque elephant man or an industrial landscape, these films show how this is possible.

In his 1990 film *Wild at Heart*, Lynch uses sound in a controversial, original, and manipulating fashion. The scene in which a black man is murdered by the protagonist, Sailor, is an example of this. A few minutes into the film, a man is paid a sum of money to kill Sailor, but sensing this, he defends himself by bashing the man's head onto the white walls of the hallway. The bashing of the head against the white wall and the splashing of the color red onto the white wall are accentuated by a sudden rupture of loud rock music. The music not only accentuates the visual aspect of the murder, but the selection of rock music even manipulates viewers into seeing Sailor not as a murderer, but as a hero.

Throughout the film, Lynch uses a sort of Brechtian *verfremdungseffekt* ("V-effect") to divide the film structure and create a moment of pause and reflection for his viewers.[115] This divisor is a single shot of a match being lit and flaring up into a fire. The scene is shot with a macro lens, which creates an extreme close-up image. Additionally, the shot is filmed in slow motion. The vertical montage here echoes the visual; it is the close recording and amplified sound of the match being lit and flaring up. Lynch uses this effect several times throughout the film.

Film director Wim Wenders uses music as an atmospheric supplement to his imagery and cinematography. In his 1984 Cannes Palme d'Or winner *Paris, Texas*, for example, the film begins with long shots of a man lost in the desert of south Texas. These shots are sometimes in silence, accentuated with natural sounds of the wind and footsteps on the road, and sometimes are filled with the film's carefully composed sound track of Ry Cooder's slide-guitar music. The music lets one note stretch out for seconds on end, thus filling the void space of the desert. The atmosphere of the Sam Shepard script highlighting the loneliness of a man wandering alone in the heat of the desert in search of his wife and child is so enormously enriched by Cooder's music that one can go as far as to consider Cooder's music as a character in the film. Depending on the scene, the tempo of Cooder's guitar changes, always remaining in tune with the spirit and atmosphere of the images, the story, and the character. It is never a hindrance, and is always a friend.

Among the films of the past two decades, *Wings of Desire* (1987), directed by Wim Wenders and cowritten by Peter Handke, stands out as a strong testimony to *mise-en-scène*. This film, winner of the 1987 Cannes Palme for Best

Director, owes much of the award to its audiovisual montage. Like *Paris, Texas*, the film largely consists of a journey. In this story, an angel desires to become a human being; he desires human love. Similar to *Paris,Texas*, and in general films about journeys, *Wings of Desire* contains an immense amount of landscape photography: buildings, ruins, rivers, skies, basements, and so on.

Just as *Paris, Texas* opens to Ry Cooder's music accompanying the landscape of south Texas, *Wings of Desire* opens with a slow panning of Berlin rooftops, a series of black and white aerial takes of Berlin, just as angels hover and thus see things from above. Once again, the usage of music is atmospheric: Wenders uses the work of composer Jurgen Knieper to create the mood and feeling of melancholy and lightness. A sense of hovering is also created through the sounds of cellos, strings, and vocals. The cello (along with the other original scores) acts as an atmospheric carrier. It fills the space above and between the Berlin buildings, while it also carries the angels from one corner to another.

Wenders also makes use of contemporary music. He has an atmospheric vocal segment composed by Laurie Anderson and a segment with live contemporary rock music. In the last moments of the film, the location shifts into a bar in the depths of Berlin, and yet we hear another atmospheric piece—this time not superimposed by vertical montage, but rather played in person by a contemporary underground band, Nick Cave and The Bad Seed. The use of contemporary music reaches its height with his next film, *Until the End of the World* (1991). In this film, Wenders uses a number of popular singers and bands, including the Talking Heads, R.E.M., U2, Lou Reed, and Peter Gabriel. The film was considered a failure by many, but nevertheless released an exceptional sound track. The use of contemporary music is a key element for him, beginning as far back as his first film *Summer in the City* (1970).[116]

As is the case with *Until the End of the World*, film sound tracks are now becoming popular albums. In an article titled "The Profit from Soundtrack Recordings Is Music to Hollywood's Ears," Jim Kotch observes that sound tracks from films are bringing in huge sums for Hollywood producers. "In the 'Billboard 200' albums chart for the week ending June 10, sixteen of the titles were motion-picture soundtracks, including two in the top ten: 'Friday,' at No. 3, and 'Forrest Gump,' at No. 6. . . . At the top of the 'Billboard Hot 100 Singles' chart was 'Have You Ever Really Loved a Woman?' by Bryan Adams, from the movie *Don Juan DeMarco*.[117] The article also observes that some film sound tracks are released even before the film has reached the screen. "Looking ahead to the week ending June 17, Mr. Adams remains atop the single chart, while the sound track to the new Walt Disney film *Pocahontas* enters the album chart at an impressive No. 4, even before the movie is due in theaters."[118] Even older film soundtracks are popular: "In addition, orchestral scores from older films like *Streetcar Named Desire* (1951) and *Giant* (1956), and even nonclassics like *King Rat* (1965) and *The Reivers* (1969), have recently been released on major labels, a sure indication of the genre's new profitability."[119] At least, with good music on the screen, filmmakers know that if their films do not last long, their sound tracks will.[120]

The use of music by many film directors, such as Lynch and Kubrick, provides not only the atmosphere and backdrop for the narrative, but also as an aftereffect—equivalent, perhaps, to Peter Brook's "burnt image" in the theater.[121] "A film is—or should be—more like music than fiction," writes Kubrick. "It should be a progression of moods and feelings. The theme, what's behind the emotion, the meaning, all comes later. After you've walked out of the theater, maybe the next day or a week later, maybe without ever actually realizing it, you somehow get what the filmmaker has been trying to tell you."[122] Thus, vertical montage, as a link to the "montage of attractions," holds an essential place in films and filmmaking.

Notes

1. Akira Kurosawa, *Something Like an Autobiography*, trans. Audie E. Bock (New York: Vintage Books Edition, 1983), 107, 191–192.

2. In many ways, montage has become an intrinsic part of our unconscious, everyday vocabulary. Without knowing it, we utilize it and long for it. Consider the following lines from a hand written letter from a freshman at the University of Michigan, Ann Arbor: "It is pretty sad, but using e-mail for so long I am finding it very difficult to write longhand. I don't think it is just with letters, but the technology of a computer: editing, cutting, pasting . . . makes it so difficult to write like this [longhand]." David Valazzi, 15 May 1995.

3. Also dean of the Irwin S. Chanin School of Architecture, Cooper Union, New York City.

4. From a lecture, "Oslo Fall Night" delivered at Columbia University, in *Columbia Documents of Architecture and Theory*, vol. II (New York: Columbia University Graduate School of Architecture, Planning and Preservation, 1993), 14.

5. Sergei Eisenstein, *Film Form*, trans. Jay Leyda (Cleveland: World Publishing Company, 1957), 48.

6. Eisenstein, *Film Form*, 28.

7. Before embarking upon filmmaking, Eisenstein was a theater director.

8. Eisenstein, *Film Form*, 15–16.

9. On a colloquial level, the Merriam-Webster's Collegiate Dictionary (10th ed.) defines "cadre" and "shot" as follows:

> **cad•re** *n* [F, fr. It *quadro,* fr. L *quadrum* square—more at QUARREL] (1830) **1** : FRAME, FRAMEWORK **2** : a nucleus or core group esp. of trained personnel able to assume control and to train others; *broadly* : a group of people having some unifying relationship <a ~ of lawyers>

> **shot** *n* [ME, fr. OE *scot,;* akin to ON *skot* shot, OHG *scuz,* OE *sceo-*
> *tan* to shoot—more at SHOOT] (bef. 12c) **1 a :** an action of shooting
> ... **8 a :** a single photographic exposure; *esp* : SNAPSHOT **b :** a sin-
> gle sequence of a motion picture or a television program shot by one
> camera without interruption

10. Eisenstein, *Film Form*, 36.

11. Frank Beaver, ed., *Dictionary of Film Terms: The Aesthetic Companion to Film
Analysis* (New York: Twayne Publishers, 1994), 311–312. The shot is also crucial within
the definition of *Shooting Script*: "Included in this production information are *shot* descriptions (scope of shot), shot numbers, location and time notations, and indications of
where special effect s are required. The director works from this script in the filming of
the story." (311).

12. Beaver, *Dictionary of Film Terms: The Aesthetic Companion to Film Analysis*,
162.

13. Jacques Aumont, *Montage/Eisenstein*, trans. Lee Hildreth, Constance Penley,
and Andrew Ross. (Bloomington, Ind.: Indiana University Press, 1987), 36.

14. André Bazin, "The Evolution of the Language of Cinema," in *What Is Cinema?*
trans. Hugh Gray (Berkeley, Ca.: University of California Press 1967), 27.

15. Bazin, "The Evolution of the Language of Cinema," 36.

16. Beaver, *Dictionary of Film Terms: The Aesthetic Companion to Film Analysis*,
163–164.

17. Eisenstein, *Film Form*, 5.

18. Eisenstein, *Film Form*, 3.

19. Eisenstein, *Film Form*, 36.

20. Eisenstein, *Film Form*, 63.

21. For a basic overview of semiotic principles, see Jonathan Culler, *Ferdinand de
Saussure* (Ithaca, N.Y.: Cornell University Press, 1986), 105–150, and Jonathan Culler,
The Pursuit of Signs: Semiotics, Literature, Deconstruction (Ithaca: Cornell University
Press, 1981).

22. Eisenstein, *Film Form*, 63.

23. Sergei Eisenstein, *Notes of a Film Director*, trans. X. Danko (London: Lawrence
and Wishart, 1959), 63.

24. Eisenstein, *Notes of a Film Director*, 63.

25. Eisenstein, *Notes of a Film Director*, 63.

26. Eisenstein, *Notes of a Film Director*, 63.

27. Eisenstein, *Film Form*, 30.

28. Eisenstein, *Film Form*, 65–66.

29. Eisenstein, *Film Form*, 49.

30. Bazin, "The Evolution of the Language of Cinema," 25.

31. Bazin, "The Evolution of the Language of Cinema," 25.

32. Bazin, "The Evolution of the Language of Cinema," 25.

33. Eisenstein, *Film Form*, 111.

34. Eisenstein, *Film Form*, 121.

35. Sergei Eisenstein, V.I. Pudovkin, and G.V. Alexandrov, "A Statement," in *Film
Form*, trans. Jay Leyda (Cleveland: World Publishing Company, 1957), 257. Here, we
find the following quote: "It is known that the basic (and only) means that has brought
the cinema to such a powerfully affective strength is MONTAGE. The affirmation of mon-

tage, as the chief means of effect, has become the indisputable axiom on which the world-wide culture of cinema has been built."

36. Bazin, "The Evolution of the Language of Cinema," 33.

37. A full analysis of Orson Welles and *Citizen Kane* will be given at length in Chapter 4. Here, we take only a quick glance to contextualize Welles with respect to the use of montage and montage theory.

38. Bazin, "The Evolution of the Language of Cinema," 33.

39. Bazin, "The Evolution of the Language of Cinema," 34.

40. Bazin, "The Evolution of the Language of Cinema," 34–35.

41. The [framed theater] of this film will be examined in detail in Chapter 4.

42. Bazin, "The Evolution of the Language of Cinema," 35.

43. Wim Wenders, *The Logic of Images: Essays and Conversations*, trans. Michael Hofmann (London: Faber and Faber, 1991), 52.

44. This is my equivalent in film language for Jacques Derrida's well-known saying, "There is nothing outside of the text."

45. The primacy of a script, preferably written by the director, is a common rule in the world of cinema today. Though many writers write the screenplay for commercial films, most first-rate directors write their own screenplays.

46. Martin Scorsese, *Scorsese on Scorsese* (London: Faber and Faber, 1989), 14.

47. Kurosawa, *Something Like an Autobiography*, 103.

48. Eisenstein, *Film Form*, 261.

49. Federico Fellini, *Comments on Film*, ed. Giovanni Grazzini, trans. Joseph Henry. (Fresno, Ca.: Press at California State University, 1988), 6–7.

50. Eisenstein, *Film Form*, 261.

51. Eisenstein, *Film Form*, 262.

52. Eisenstein, *Film Form*, 262.

53. The most notable example is the collaboration between Bertolt Brecht and the designer Caspar Neher.

54. Ingmar Bergman, *Bergman on Bergman* (London: Secker and Warburg, 1973), 97.

55. Scorsese, *Scorsese on Scorsese*, 54.

56. François Truffaut, "Foreword," in *Orson Welles*, ed. André Bazin, trans. Jonathan Rosenbaum (New York: Harper & Row, 1978), 7.

57. Bazin, André, *Orson Welles*, trans. Jonathan Rosenbaum (New York: Harper and Row, 1978), 21.

58. Kurosawa, *Something Like an Autobiography*, 104.

59. Fellini, *Comments on Film*, 223.

60. Bergman, *Bergman on Bergman*, 209.

61. Fellini, *Comments on Film*, 223.

62. Kurosawa, *Something Like an Autobiography*, 197–198.

63. Kurosawa, *Something Like an Autobiography*, 105.

64. Wenders, *The Logic of Images*, 5.

65. Kurosawa, *Something Like an Autobiography*, 105–106.

66. Although the general rule of filmmaking and montage is to lead the film towards fluidity—much like Kurosawa's "deep river"—there are also filmmakers who have made a reputation not only by breaking this rule, but by consciously going against it. The most notable such director is Jean-Luc Godard. Many of Godard's films are purely theatrical and cerebral games with montage theory. Often, his films have no narrative, no begin-

ning, and no end. They are simply thoughts fleshed out on screen and juxtaposed with one another with different layerings of sound, music, and text. The lyricism of Godard's films, if there is any, lies precisely in this: It is all montage without formal structure. It is the montage itself that we watch on screen, not a story or a narrative. His cinema is one in which the invisible montage is made visible. The action–reaction between Bergman and Godard is worth noting. In 1958, *Cahiers du Cinéma*, Godard wrote an article on Bergman's *Summer Interlude*, titled "Bergmanorama." He writes: "The cinema is not a craft. It is an art. It does not mean teamwork. One is always alone; on the set as before the blank. And for Bergman, to be alone means to ask questions. And to make films means to answer them. Nothing could be more classically romantic." To this Bergman responds: "I find Godard's way of putting things bewitching. It's precisely what he does himself, what he has fallen victim to! He's writing about himself," (*Bergman on Bergman,* 60.) To defend himself, Bergman continues by paying respect to the theater: "You must never forget that my life has been lived in the theater; and theater—even if it's a protected world—is always a collective. Producing a play, one belongs in high degree to a group. (*Bergman on Bergman,* 61.) Elsewhere, Bergman on Godard remarks: "Hell, but Godard's morals must be low!" (*Bergman on Bergman,* 208).

67. Kurosawa, *Something Like an Autobiography,* 113.

68. Wenders, *The Logic of Images,* 33.

69. Frederico Fellini, "The birth of a film," in *Fellini on Fellini,* eds. Anna Keel and Christian Strich, trans. Isabel Quigley (New York: Dell Publishing Company, Inc., 1976), 165.

71. Bergman, *Bergman on Bergman,* 209.

71. Bergman, *The Magic Lantern,* trans. Joan Tate (New York: Viking, 1988), 73.

72. Bergman, *Bergman on Bergman,* 166.

73. Bergman, *Bergman on Bergman,* 162.

74. Bergman, *The Magic Lantern,* 73.

75. Kurosawa, *Something Like an Autobiography,* 193.

76. Bergman, *Bergman on Bergman,* 181.

77. Bergman, *The Magic Lantern,* 243.

78. Bergman, *The Magic Lantern,* 243.

79. Kurosawa, *Something Like an Autobiography,* 191–192.

80. Kurosawa, *Something Like an Autobiography,* 107.

81. Eisenstein, *Film Form,* 45.

82. Eisenstein, *Film Form,* 92.

83. Eisenstein, *Film Form,* 70–71.

84. Eisenstein, *Film Form,* 71.

85. Eisenstein, *Film Form,* 254.

86. Eisenstein, *Film Sense,* 69.

87. Eisenstein, *Film Sense,* 70.

88. Eisenstein, *Film Sense,* 70.

89. Eisenstein, *Film Sense,* 74.

90. Eisenstein, *Film Sense,* 75.

91. Eisenstein, *Film Sense,* 78.

92. Eisenstein, *Film Sense,* 79.

93. Eisenstein, *Film Sense,* 77.

94. Eisenstein, *Film Sense,* 168.

95. Scorsese, *Scorsese on Scorsese,* 8.

96. Heiner Müller, *Germania,* ed. Sylvère Lotringer, trans. Bernard and Caroline Schütze (New York: Semiotext[e], 1990), 165.

97. Wenders, *The Logic of Images,* 36.

98. Scorsese, *Scorsese on Scorsese,* 45.

99. Kurosawa, *Something Like an Autobiography,* 186.

100. Kurosawa, *Something Like an Autobiography,* 186.

101. Scorsese, *Scorsese on Scorsese,* 45.

102. Fellini, *Comments on Film,* 223.

103. Fellini, *Comments on Film,* 223.

104. Fellini, *Comments on Film,* 223.

105. Fellini, *Fellini on Fellini,* 109.

106. Fellini, *Fellini on Fellini,* 110.

107. Fellini, *Fellini on Fellini,* 109.

108. Kurosawa, *Something Like an Autobiography,* 197.

109. Kurosawa, *Something Like an Autobiography,* 197.

110. Norman Kagan, *The Cinema of Stanley Kubrick* (New York: Grove Press, Inc., 1972), 169.

111. Kurosawa, *Something Like an Autobiography,* 108.

112. Kurosawa, *Something Like an Autobiography,* 108.

113. Kurosawa, *Something Like an Autobiography,* 197.

114. Scorsese, *Scorsese on Scorsese,* 83.

115. See Chapter 1, page 21 for a definition of *verfremdungseffekt.*

116. According to Wenders, this film came out of his desire to use his (then) top-ten choices of songs on the screen. See Wenders, *Logic of Images,* 90.

117. Jim Kotch, "The Profit From Soundtrack Recordings Is Music to Hollywood's Ears," *New York Times,* 12 June, 1995, 5(B).

118. Kotch, "The Profit from Soundtrack Recordings Is Music to Hollywood's Ears," 5(B).

119. Kotch, "The Profit from Soundtrack Recordings Is Music to Hollywood's Ears," 5(B).

120. The same is true for the theater. Often, if a scene is not working, and cannot be made to work, the director adds music to compensate for the poor acting or poor staging.

121. See Chapter 1, note 40.

122. Kagan, *The Cinema of Stanley Kubrick,* 189.

Chapter 4
Unfolding the [Frame]:
The Cinematic Theater

Cinema and theater are two means of conveying a story . . . their difference is
exactly the same as that of a watercolor painting and an oil painting: in film
you use no oil, in theater you use no water.

—Liviu Ciulei[1]

The [Framed Theater]

Having examined montage, in both theory and practice, we are now ready to
apply it to the theater stage, to transfigure the theatrical time and space into a
cinematic one. To do this, however, I begin by examining the inverse process,
namely the importing and framing of theater into the frame of cinema.

This process was first introduced and developed by Orson Welles, a theater
director who turned to film. I call this process of bringing the theater into films
[framed theater]—"framed" because it is the *cadre* of a camera viewing and
shooting the scene, and "theater" because it is a series of scenes built into a single moment, as in the theater.[2] Instead of dividing the scene into segments and
pasting them to one another through montage, the [framed theater] creates, for
the camera frame, a single unit from a series of scenes. With this distinction
defined, the *cinematic stage* is none other than the inverse of the [framed thea-
ter]:

> Theater to Cinema: cinematic stage <——— [framed theater]
> Cinema to Theater: [framed theater] ———> cinematic stage

To describe this process of inversing the [framed theater], it is best to begin with
an examination of Orson Welles and his creation of the [framed theater] through

97

his experience as a radio and theater director.

In 1937, at the age of twenty-two, Welles formed his own theater company, The Mercury Theater, and with this ensemble proceeded to stage a grand diversity of world classics at a very rapid rate: *Julius Caesar* in 1937; Bernard Shaw's *Heartbreak House* in 1938; Büchner's *Danton's Death* in 1938; and a disastrous theatrical collage of *Richard II*, *Henry IV*, *Henry V*, *Henry V*, and *Richard III* titled *Five Kings*. *Five Kings* never opened and its non-opening marked the end of Welles' theater company. Though short lived, "Mercury had played a major role in the prewar American theater and its influence could be compared to that of the Cartel in France."[3]

Simultaneous with his theater work, and as early as 1938, Welles also broadcast radio plays on a weekly basis for CBS Radio, in a program called "The Mercury Theater on the Air." Again, the program featured classics—both plays as well as novels—adapted for the radio: *Treasure Island*, *Jane Eyre*, *The Man Who Was Thursday*, *Julius Caesar*, *Around the World in 80 Days*, and several others. In his critical study, *Orson Welles*, Bazin notes that "the theater not only precedes cinema for the director of *Citizen Kane* and *Othello*, but profoundly and essentially conditions all the manifestations of Welles' genius, the cinema first of all."[4] The same holds true of his radio experience.

The world of cinema (Hollywood) first discovered Welles through a contagious event that took place on October 30, 1938, as a result of one of his radio-play broadcasts, *The War of the Worlds*. While rehearsing *Danton's Death*, the day before this event, the ensemble listened to a trial run of their next day's broadcast. Disappointed with their boring and dry performances, they decided to liven it up by accentuating the realism of the portrayed events. Welles "spent the night revising the adaptation by situating the action in different parts of America. Nevertheless, the results didn't look like much, and this was also the opinion of all those who heard the final rehearsal, actors and technicians alike. But it was too late to make improvements."[5] The next day, however, the broadcast shocked and spread a vast panic all over America.[6]

Following this "spectacular" event—a scandal, a disaster, and a triumph all in one—Welles' first customer was none other than the filmmaking industry itself: Hollywood's RKO Pictures, Inc. To sign a contract, Welles wanted complete freedom—an unheard of request (and taboo) in the filmmaking industry.[7] In August 1939, after months of negotiation, RKO agreed to a carte blanche: complete artistic and production freedom, with no intervention from the producers, the cast of actors from The Mercury Theater ensemble, and a decent salary. One year after his arrival in Hollywood, *The Motion Picture Herald* headlined: "Silence! Genius at Work."[8]

Again, to stress an important fact, *Citizen Kane* was Welles' first film-directing experience.[9] Before this revolutionary film, his directing experience was purely through his theater and radio work with his Mercury Theater ensemble. As an artist therefore, his directing vocabulary was rich in spatial and visual composition, text analysis, sound, and music. What he lacked was the cinematic language: the language and art of cinematography and montage. His cinematic naiveté was such that on his first visit to RKO studios, he exclaimed, "This is the biggest electric train set any boy ever had!" A single important question remained: How should he play with his huge electric train set?[10] During the delays of 1939–1940, Welles took the time to explore the studio's equipment, the rules and regulations of filming, and the art of montage. Meanwhile, he supplemented his technical education with film screenings: He had the RKO Studios screen him film after film. In this manner, Welles taught himself—better than any film school could possibly do—the art of filmmaking. When it was time to start shooting, Welles the theater-radio director had metamorphosed into a well-equipped film director. The shooting of *Citizen Kane* lasted fifteen weeks, and the film was ready for montage on October 23, 1940.

If this film was very revolutionary for its time, and still remains so, it is because Welles broke every rule he could. He broke all standards of scriptwriting, filming, shooting, and editing. The revolution of Orson Welles was at once brave in its risk taking, and highly calculated in its actualization. Having had the liberty of seeing as many films as he wanted to see, Welles had come to learn the classic laws of scriptwriting and montage. He knew, therefore, exactly what the laws were, and with his solid theater background and rich sensitivity, he was well equipped to break these laws.

Today, over half a century later, the film still endures as the "best film ever made."[11] Orson Welles' youthful experiment with form—with the "cinematic form"—was to renovate lost and marginalized techniques, while giving birth to new ones.

To begin with: the script.

The script, a semi-fictional biography of William Randolph Hearst, did not respect chronology whatsoever. Up until *Citizen Kane*, the current logic of a narrative, especially a biographical one, had been linear: It would start with "A" and chronologically proceed until it would reach its final destination of "Z." Rather than narrating the film in such fashion—in a linear sequence—Welles renovated the old technique of "flashback," and fully exploited it to construct his entire film, the entire life of his hero, Citizen Kane.

The technique of flashback was not original in 1941. It had been used, for example, in Marcel Carné's *Le Jour se Lève* (1939). As Bazin points out: "Welles is not really the inventor of this in the cinema, and the procedure was obviously taken from novels. But he perfected its use and adapted it to the resources of cinema with a comprehensiveness that had never yet been achieved."[12] This being said, no other film before *Citizen Kane* (or even post-*Citizen Kane*!) had ever used the flashback with such a strategy and a strong force to create a revolution through the narrative. "In any case," Bazin remarks, "if Welles did not actually invent the flashback, his film introduced it into the current cinema language. The history of scriptwriting was incontestably turned topsy-turvy by it."[13]

The best analogy to illustrate the nature of his script is a jigsaw puzzle. Before *Citizen Kane*, narratives were predominantly constructed in a linear manner. Welles, on the other hand, created an entire jigsaw puzzle, fitting each piece of the portrait in a different location on the board—each and every piece constructing and leading to the final picture, the final portrait of Kane's life. His idea for such a script was a revolutionary one, but now it also needed a structure—a frame—to contain his jigsaw puzzle portrait.[14]

The solution for the frame was as brilliant as the script itself. A group of reporters embark on discovering the meaning of Kane's last words. This framing device was used in the opening scene as a launching pad into the entire jigsaw puzzle construction of the film. Consider the following opening shots of the film: 1) a dreamlike sequence unveils Kane's kingdom, with Kane's old voice pronouncing (as he dies) the word "Rosebud!"; 2) a projection room with a "News on the March" documentary reel unveils Kane's life to a group of reporters; and 3) upon seeing the film, the reporters now want to discover what Kane's last word, "Rosebud," meant. The dialogue in the last shot of the opening sequence frames the inquiry/journey for us.

The script-made-into-a-film by Welles is so perfectly complete, detailed, and complicated in its *mise-en-cadre* and *mise-en-scène* that no matter how many times the film is seen, it will not exhaust itself. There is never a possibility of memorizing this film. As Truffaut remarks: "When I see *Kane* today, I'm aware that I know it by heart, but in the way you know a recording rather than a movie. I'm not always as certain what image comes next as I am about what sound will burst forth, or the very timbre of the next voice that I am going to hear, or the musical link to the next scene."[15] The musical linking of the scenes was a technique that Welles borrowed from his theater. In his *Voodoo Macbeth*, for example, "Music was integral to transitions from one scene to the next. During a ballroom scene in this film, while lords and ladies danced to a medley of Joseph Lanner waltzes, drumbeats began quietly to intrude on these genteel proceedings, reaching their crescendo after the image of dancers within the palace had transformed, in a manner reminiscent of a film dissolve, to that of Hecate standing silhouetted by a "strange light" let in through the open palace gates."[16]

The inexhaustibility of *Citizen Kane's mise-en-cadre* arises from its rich and varied background of theater and radio productions. Being a director of theater-radio productions, Welles emphasized the ignored and marginalized elements of the cinema, namely sound and music, and centralized them. For Welles, the final product of a shot (before it was filmed) was the combination: [*visual composition + detailed sound*]. For the creator of theater-radio productions, the sound track was an integral part of the film event: sound and the visual frame could not exist apart from one another in the shot. They needed to have the same level of importance. Joseph McBride attested to this fact when he wrote of the early days of Welles' directing: "In the course of numerous preliminary rehearsals with his actors, Orson had recorded all the film's dialogue with the intention of shooting the entire film to synchronize with the playback. After shooting started he had to give up this idea, which presented too many technical difficulties for the actors."[17]

Regarding the importance of vertical montage and the revolutionary usage of sound and music by Orson Welles, Truffaut observes that: "(Before Kane, nobody in Hollywood knew how to set music properly in movies.) Kane was the first, in fact the only, great film that uses radio techniques. Behind each scene, there is a resonance which gives it its color: the rain on the windows of the cabaret, 'El Rancho,' when the investigator goes to visit the down-and-out female singer who can only 'work' Atlantic City; the echoes in the marble-lined Thatcher library; the overlapping voices wherever there are several characters."[18]   Truffaut concludes: "A lot of filmmakers know enough to follow Auguste Renoir's advice to fill the eyes with images at all costs, but only Orson Welles understood that the sound track had to be filled in the same way."[19]

The privileging of sound in the frame by no means took away from the visual aspect of the shot. It remained as important as ever. Sound is considered a crucial supplement to the image, highlighting the visual in the most subtle manner. "It will frequently be noted that Welles takes paradoxical care to have the most important lines uttered precisely when the actor is least visible."[20] Voice, sound, and music all combined to create a super-saturated and super-structured sound track: "Here, in Kane, we have a film where the voices count as much as words, dialogue which has characters speaking at the same time like musical instruments in a score, with sentences left unfinished as in life."[21] This mastery of language and sound is a skill that Welles learned from his years as a radio-play director/actor.[22]

From the radio, he also imported one of the crucial marvels of sound for the film: the use of vertical montage so the audio track would not be left out of transitions. "His radio experience taught him never to leave a film in repose, to set up aural bridges from one scene to the next, making use of music as no one had before him, to capture or stimulate awareness, to play with the volume of voices at least as much as the words."[23] Film, for Welles, rather than being a "plastic object," is "duration, something which unwinds like a ribbon," much like "a ribbon of dreams."[24]

"We must not forget," concludes Truffaut, "that where the silent cinema gave us great visual talents—Murnau, Eisenstein, Dryer, Hitchcock—the sound cinema has given us only one, one single filmmaker whose style is immediately recognizable after three minutes of film, and his name is Orson Welles."[25] This being the case, it is important to note that Welles does not privilege one element over another. In his cinema, there is no center. Sound, for example, is as central as the image. In fact, one can argue that in the Wellesian frames, the scenes are focused around sound.

Focusing the scene around the sound is a technique that Welles brought into the cinema from the theater. In the theater, "the entire work is presented to you on a tray."[26] Thus, you have a single space (one stage) in which you do not have the advantage of camera point of view, camera perspective, or montage to communicate and design your scene. Everything takes place in one space. This being the case, the stage director has to take an infinite amount of care to focus his or her scene in order to focus the spectator's eyes. Thus, the task of focus in theater, is of primary importance to composition—audio and visual—and the *mise-en-scène*. Here is a concrete example: You can have the main hero committing suicide center stage with a full spotlight on him. But, if in the upper right hand corner of the stage, you have another actor tying his shoelace with a small distraction, for instance, small sounds, the audience inevitably will look at the second actor![27]

Well aware of this mechanism of theatrical focus, Welles used sound, instead of the camera, to focus his audience's attention. He set the scene, as in the theater, and guided the focus with emphasis on the different sound planes. This Wellesian signature becomes even more significant when he broke the montage theory by placing a fixed camera, with a depth of focus, into the scene and letting the scene run its course in the frame—thereby creating a [framed theater]. Such Welles scenes were carefully staged theater as framed through the in-depth-focus lens of a camera. The positioning of the camera for his "depth of field" shot was also a location that Welles brought over from the theater. Truffaut notes: "Orson Welles' favorite angle led him to place the camera on the ground, but doesn't that bring him by the same token to present his protagonists as we would see them in the theater if we were seated in the first ten rows of the orchestra?"[28]

Such an import from the theater into the cinema created a revolution. His framed scenes did away with montage and returned the cinema back to the theater. "Thanks to the depth of field, all of the actors participate in the action and the entire set, including the ceilings, encloses them in its presence."[29] Doing away with montage forced the framed scene to return to the theater. The scene was carefully placed on stage [*mise-en-scène*], carefully placed in the frame [*mise-en-cadre*], carefully rehearsed, and finally shot with full sound and music.

> It is possible, for example, to suppose that Welles, as a man of the theater, constructs his mise-en-scène on the basis of the actor. One may imagine that the intuition of the sequence shot, this new unit in film semantics and syntax, grew out of a vision of a director accustomed to placing the actor within the décor, who experienced traditional editing no longer as a fluency or language but as a loss of efficacy, a mutilation of the spectacular possibilities of the image. For Welles, each scene to be played forms a complete unit in time and space.[30]

Indeed montage is defined by cutting and uniting—a process that is rarely needed in the theater since the stage has a built-in time–space continuity. To apply montage to the stage would perhaps create an unnecessary "mutilation"; it would destroy the fluidity of the image. On the other hand, to replace montage with a depth of focus involves nothing else but replacing a set of shots with a continuous take of a single scene, yielding a framed scene, a framed theater, or a filmed theater. Bazin continues to describe the theater-like continuity of time and space in Welles' *mise-en-cadre*:

> The acting loses its meaning, is deprived of its dramatic blood like a severed limb, if it ceases to maintain a living and responsive connection with the other characters and the décor. Furthermore, the scene charges itself like an electrical condenser as it progresses and must be kept carefully insulated against all parasitic contacts until a sufficient dramatic voltage has been reached, which produces the spark that all the action has been directed towards.[31]

The impact of Welles' import of theater into the cinema is most visible in his *mise-en-scène* of scenes. Welles created a staged scene, and rather than cutting it into pieces, he framed it with a fixed camera, and let the camera roll nonstop. Action, sound, and text all merged in this framed shot:

> Take, for instance, Welles' favorite scene in *The Magnificent Ambersons*: the one in the kitchen between Fanny and George and, later, Jack. It lasts almost the length of an entire reel of film.[32] The camera remains immobile from start to finish, facing Fanny and George; the latter, having just returned from a trip with his mother, has rushed into the kitchen to gorge himself on strawberry shortcake prepared by his aunt.[33]

To look more carefully at another example of Welles' [framed theater], consider Susan's attempted suicide in *Citizen Kane*. As written in the shooting script, labeled scene #94, the scene shows the interior of Susan's bedroom in Kane's home, on a late night in 1920. In this shot, the camera is positioned at the opposite side of the room from the entrance. The frame contains a bedside table with medication and a glass with a spoon, behind which Susan is sleeping on a bed. Using depth of field, the frame also focuses on a door on the far side of the bedroom, beyond Susan. The sound plane for this shot consists of Susan breathing heavily, and Kane's and Joseph's voices and their knocking on the door. As Susan does not reply, they break in. The door crashes and we see the two figures rush into the bedroom. Kane rushes into the bedroom, kneels at Susan's bed, and reaches for her forehead.[34]

As written in the script, the director would have an infinite number of ways to shoot and stage this scene. For example, through montage theory, the scene could have easily been cut and shot as follows:

> shot of Susan in the bed—a closeup of Susan's face; sound of her breathing; sound of the door knocking—shot of the door—shot of Susan in bed breathing;

knocking on the door—shot of door with the dialogue in the back—shot of Susan; dialogue continuation; sound of the crash of the door—shot of Kane and Joseph in the door frame; rushing of Kane towards Susan (the camera)—shot of Susan, as taken from behind Kane—close-up of Susan—shot of Kane beside the bed, from front angle; dialogue "Get Dr. Corey."—Joseph's exit.[35]

Figure 4.1 shows what Welles himself did with this scene. He did away with montage, and like a stage director in the audience seat, he located the camera at the corner of the room, framing the entire scene through one depth-of-field shot, constituting a [framed theater]. The entire scene played out nonstop, without any cuts, as in the theater, and was filmed in a single shot. In the continuity script,[36] the scene appears with the same emphasis on depth of field and the sound plane.[37]

Figure 4.1. Susan's suicide. CITIZEN KANE © 1941 RKO Pictures, Inc. All Rights Reserved.

To obtain a full appreciation for the theatrical nature of the *mise-en-scène* of this scene, along with its continuity in time and space, consider the following description by André Bazin:

The scene opens on Susan's bedroom seen from behind the night table. In close-up, wedged against the camera, is an enormous glass, taking up almost a quarter of the image, along with a little spoon and an open medicine bottle. The glass almost entirely conceals Susan's bed, enclosed in a shadowy zone from which only a faint sound of labored breathing escapes, like that of a drugged sleeper. The bedroom is empty; far away in the background of this private desert is the door, rendered even far more distant by the lens' false perspectives, and, behind the door, a knocking. Without having seen anything but a glass and heard two noises, on two different sound planes, we have immediately grasped the situation: Susan has locked herself in her room to try to kill herself; Kane is trying to get in.[38]

Before continuing with the analysis of the scene, it is important to note again that Welles' *mise-en-scène* is a direct derivation of his experience in the theater space. If the art of films is composition through montage, the art of theater consists of composition in space. How, for example, can Hedda Gabler's suicide be staged? Using the depth of field, Welles opted for shooting scenes through a [framed-theater] rather than through montage.

The effect of Welles' import of the theater onto the screen can be stunning. It can easily create the entire scope of emotions without using montage. For example, the [framed theater] scenes can be shocking (as previously described scene), or horrific (as used in *The Trial*), or simply sad. A good example can be found early on in *Citizen Kane*, in which Mr. Thatcher comes to Kane family's boardinghouse to take young Charles Kane away. The well-composed frame shows the interior of the house, with Mrs. Kane and Thatcher sitting behind a table, close to the camera, reviewing and signing the agreement. Mr. Kane is standing up a bit further down from the table looking at them, (the ceiling of the house can be seen). Brilliantly enough, at the back wall, there is a window, through which we see young Kane making a snowman (the snow being an important friend to Rosebud). The juxtaposition of the two visual planes, one about playful and joyful youth, with the other about the selling of this youth, exposed side by side, simultaneously, is perhaps one of the most heart-wrenching moments in the film. The effect could never have ever been achieved as efficiently and immediately by any form of montage.

Welles turned his [framed theater] into film through his extraordinary understanding and usage of vertical montage. His usage of the sound track—the vertical montage of sound+dialogue+words—on top of the scene creates and focuses the entire scene, and is essential to the framed tableau. Again, in relation to the scene of Susan's attempted suicide:

> The scene's dramatic structure is basically founded on the distinction between the two sound planes: close up, Susan's breathing, and from behind the door, her husband's knocking. A tension is established between these two poles, which are kept at a distance from each other by the deep focus. Now the knocks become louder; Kane is trying to force the door with his shoulder; he succeeds. We see him appear, tiny, framed in the doorway, and then rush toward us. The spark has been ignited between the two dramatic poles of the image. The scene is over.[39]

Where Eisenstein gave us the law of montage [frame and shoot, cut and paste in sequence], Welles gave us the liberty of breaking this law [frame and shoot; and keep on shooting]. Welles' [framed theater] bravely does away with montage, which narrates through frame by frame, shot by shot. Instead, it establishes one scene, frames it, and then shoots it while placing emphasis on the sound plane and the vertical montage.

The impact of Welles' experiment carries through to the present day. If today we have filmmakers such as Jim Jarmusch, whose films, such as *Down by Law* (1986) and *Stranger Than Paradise* (1985), consist of a series framed scenes, each with a long duration, it is thanks to Welles breaking the standard law of montage with *Citizen Kane* and creating the [framed theater]. Wim Wenders happily places his camera in one spot for minutes on end: "There's a shot in it (*Summer in the City* [1970]) of a cinema in Berlin and it is held for two minutes without anything happening, just because I happened to like the cinema. . . . Or we drove the length of Kudamm, shooting out of the car window. In the film that lasts eight minutes, just as long as it took to shoot."[40] If today we have directors such as Robert Altman, who opened *The Player* (1992) with a single, five-minute panning shot,[41] or Alexander Sokurov who made *The Russian Ark* (2002) in one single take, without any cuts, for ninety minutes, then it is once again thanks to Welles' *Citizen Kane*.[42] The debt of contemporary cinema to Welles and his [framed theater] is immense.

Though Welles favored the [framed theater] over the montage, he nevertheless did not do away with it completely. In fact, like all other film directors, he used montage to create his vision for the screen. Truffaut points out that even as early as *Citizen Kane*, Welles cleverly and shrewdly used montage to turn the film into an extravaganza: "The truth is that *Citizen Kane* is a film that if not cheap was at least modest, and was made to look sumptuous on the cutting-room table. This result was achieved by an enormous amount of work to enhance all the separate elements, and especially through the extraordinary strengthening of the visual track by the most ingenious sound in the history of movies."[43]

It is therefore both unfair and incorrect to claim that Welles did away with montage, or that he abolished the law of montage. In his own naive manner, he simply appeared on the cinema scene and did what he knew best: radio and theater plays. He emphasized the sound and vertical montage, and took the risk of creating scenes with a single shot through the depth of field. This had never been done before. Nor did anyone else have the courage or the suitable background to risk such an experiment. No film, not even *Citizen Kane*, can therefore do away with montage because montage *is* the single most important aspect of the cinema. It is what finally gives it its shape, its life, and its form.

Truffaut gives the best summary of Welles' use of montage in *Citizen Kane* when he writes: "The films of Orson Welles are shot by an exhibitionist and cut by a censor."[44] Welles exposes the scene, frames it, has a long shot, and then mercilessly and accurately cuts all that is unnecessary and unwanted. As Welles became a more experienced filmmaker, the role of montage gained a higher degree of importance. In 1952, with his film of *Othello*, for example, montage was to save him.

Othello, which was presented at the 1952 Cannes Festival as a Moroccan film and shared the Grand Prix with Renato Castellani's *Two Cent's Worth of Hope*, was entirely constructed through montage. Different scenes were shot in different locations, and sometimes the same scene was shot in two different locations. With the help of camera angles and montage, however, the audience would never realize the difference. Welles makes an amusing confession regarding the shooting and montage of *Othello*: "Every time you see someone with his back turned or with a hood over his head, you can be sure that it's a stand-in. I had to do everything by cross cutting because I was never able to get Iago, Desdemona and Roderigo, etc., together at once in front of the camera."[45] Attesting to the mastery of montage by Welles in *Othello*, Truffaut remarks, "Only the very great technician that he was from the beginning could have brought it off, and there is no doubt that in editing this film which comprises nearly two thousand shots (*Citizen Kane* had only 562, *Ambersons* probably only half that many), Welles became passionately involved with this stage of filmmaking."[46]

Montage is therefore essential, even for the director of *Citizen Kane*. Yet, through Welles, the elements that he brought from his theater and radio directing—sound, music, vertical montage, and timing—gained an equal level of importance in cinema. With *Citizen Kane*, Welles started off by framing the scenes and shooting them. By the time of *Othello*, he composed through montage. "Welles has always been a musical director, but before *Othello* he created music *within* the shots. Starting with *Othello*, he would make music at the editing table, that is to say, *between* the shots."[47]

Composing between the shots is precisely the art of montage, and the art that needs to be applied to the stage. Consider Welles' commentary on the role of montage in filmmaking:

> Editing is essential for the director; it's the only time he has complete control over the form of his film. When I shoot, the sun dictates certain things that I can't fight against, the actor makes certain things happen that I have to adapt to, and the story does this as well; I only concentrate on mastering what I can. The one place where I exercise absolute control is in the editing room; it is only then that the director has the power of a true artist. . . . I search for the precise rhythm between one shot and the next. It's a question of the ear: editing is the moment when the film involves a sense of hearing. . . . I work very slowly at the editing table, which always has the effect of incurring the wrath of the producers, who snatch the film from my hands. I don't know why it takes me so long; I could work forever on the editing of a film. What interests me is that strip of celluloid is performed like a musical score, and this performance is determined by the editing, just as one conductor will interpret a piece of music

completely in rubato, another will play it in a very dry and academic way, still another will do it very romantically, and so on. The images themselves aren't enough; they are always very important, but they are only images. The essential thing is the duration of each image, what follows each image; it's the whole eloquence of cinema that one is putting together in an editing room.[48]

Cinematic Theater and Its Stage

What remains to be done is to bring the editing room to the theater to apply montage theory to the stage, and, ultimately, to reverse the Wellesian [framed theater] and return the theater on screen back to the stage. This reversal of the [framed theater] will yield the cinematic stage. In other words,

cinematic stage = [montage of attractions + vertical montage]

Let us now unfold the [framed theater] and see what the result—the cinematic stage—is like. Considering Eisenstein's diagram of montage (Figure 3.2) and our discussion of both vertical and horizontal montage, we can unwind the "ribbon of dreams" and transfigure it, or map it, onto the space of a stage. Mathematically, the process involves moving from $[R^2+t]$ to $[R^3+t]$, where R^2 represents a space of two dimensions, R^3 is a space of three dimensions, and t is time.

The starting point for this process will be the script. As previously discussed in Chapter 2, the cinematic structure is similar to the epic structure in that the script needs to be broken down into tableaux, each of which can stand on its own, by itself, independent of the tableaux to its left and right. Together, as a unit in time, the succession of tableaux creates a "visual track."

Each tableau within this sequence will then have to be transformed and developed to have its own texture, its own life, and its own color. This involves the visual composition on stage through sets, costumes, blocking, and lighting, as well as rhythm, tempo, movement, and the pacing. This will be the framing of the tableaux.

Upon framing of the scene, the tableaux need to be ordered in a sequence to yield the narrative. The sequence can be linear or it can be nonlinear, as in the case of *Citizen Kane*. As each scene can stand on its own, independent of the previous one or the following one, the sequencing should be arranged to yield the greatest amount of clarity and enjoyment in the narrative.

Such a definition and framing of the tableaux, combined with the creation of a visual track—first on paper and then on stage—is then the equivalent in theater of the cinematic notion of visual montage, or montage of attractions.

[] []
visual track

Figure 4.2. Diagram of tableau sequencing for "montage of attractions" (visual montage).

The next step is the "vertical montage," or the one-to-one correlation between the "sound track" and the "visual track." In the same way that each scene has its own visual texture and tone, each scene will also need its visual equivalent in sound. The sound track includes the sounds in the scene and the music, as well as the amplified, or prerecorded, spoken text. The audio track will then, also, determine the length of the staged film—the unwounded "ribbon of dreams." Figure 4.3 charts the one-to-one vertical montage.

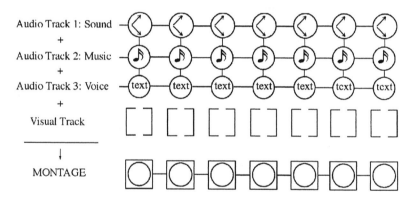

Audio Track 1: Sound
+
Audio Track 2: Music
+
Audio Track 3: Voice
+
Visual Track

↓

MONTAGE

Figure 4.3. Diagram of vertical montage.

By unfolding the [framed theater], the theater stage is transfigured into a cinematic stage. The following two principles, derived from montage theory and spatial transfiguration, are the basis for the cinematic theater's form and structure.

1. Rooted in the auteur-director tradition of both the cinema and the theater, the director is responsible for the screenplay/script. If not the original writer, the director should, when necessary, rearrange, restructure, and style the text, based on the framing and sequencing of tableaux. (Bergman's montage through filming and Kurosawa's "symphonic structure" are prime examples.) Each visual frame and sequence (montage of attraction) also needs to have a one-to-one audio track (vertical montage). This includes the spoken text, sounds, and music. The combination of the audio

and the visual track compose the cinematic stage and its tableaux. The sum of such tableaux in a well ordered sequence constructs the narrative onstage within a given fixed time t.

2. To create a cinematic stage for the cinematic theater, the stage and its surrounding space are transformed into a distanced, single-unit, panoptic space. This transfiguration is created through the fold and *Raum*.

From the preceding two principles, the following properties are derived for the cinematic theater:

1. After the montage is completed and a visual track is set, the vertical montage is created for the sequence of frames. The microphoned (or prerecorded) dialogue, mixed with the combination of sounds and music, can be called the *sound track* or *audio track*. The sound track is accorded the same level of importance as the text. As in the cinema, the sound track will be heard through the speakers, and thus the audio of the cinematic theater will be *distanced*.

2. A consequence of this sound track will be a *fixed time*, t, of the stage and its performance. As in the cinema, the time will now be fixed, and the stage will have to adhere to the rigor of every second, keeping up with every step and moment. This has already been discussed with respect to the works of Robert Wilson and Richard Foreman in Chapter 1.

3. The space is transfigured into a cinematic space with a fold and a *Raum*, such that the visuals of the cinematic theater, or the visual track, are also *distanced*. While the *Raum* will create and contain a fully autonomous space for the cinematic theater reality, the frame and the screen will fully enclose and seal this reality. The frame and the screen will also limit the spectator's view of the space/room.

4. Within the *Raum,* which is precisely defined both in space as well as time (by the sound track), precision of blocking is extremely important. Given this fact, the standard blocking vocabulary of "upstage right" and "downstage left" will not be rigorous enough. Replacing this standard vocabulary of blocking with that of the *Cartesian plane (R3) plus time (t),* the director can coordinate and position everything in a precise manner with respect to both space as well as time.

5. The *Raum,* located behind the screen of the frame, can also be placed on a rotating stage. In this manner, the standard fixed point of view of a theater can be broken into *variable points of view.* Just as the film camera is ca-

pable of viewing and shooting a scene from a variety of perspectives and angles, a rotating scene can achieve the same in theater. Thus, by rotating the stage, a variety of points of view can be seen through the frame.

6. Within this self-contained unit, the audio track can easily fill and govern the space. Therefore, the Raum can also act as a sound environment. In this manner, *counterpoint* of music/movement can also be implemented. Movement, for example, can be coordinated and choreographed to create a cinematic slow motion.

7. In the cinematic theater space, the cinematic stage should be located and placed at a distance from the spectators' seats, as in a cinema. For the cinematic theater reality to be closer to the film reality (as opposed to the theater), it needs to create an illusion that the actions have already been filmed and are being projected now. The closer the actors are to the audience, the closer they are to revealing their theatrical presence. The further they are from the audience, the more of an illusion will be created; the audience will recognize at once that the stage they are watching is located in the present, but due to the audio and visual distancing, they will have to confront the distance. *What they will be watching is a paradox: The cinematic theater is at once in the present time, and has presence, and is located in a time and space of non-presence.* This is the single most important achievement of the cinematic theater.

8. As a consequence of this setup—the single-unit panoptic apparatus—the audience will believe that they are seeing a *living cinema*. The paradoxical illusion, or rather, the reality of the living cinema, should not be broken at all until the very end, when the audience exits the theater space. At all times, the cinematic reality must confront the audience: "This is a film you are seeing and not a play! This is the cinema you are in and not the theater!" To move in this direction, the actors should have no curtain call, but rather remain backstage while credits are being projected onto the screen, preferably along with theme music from the production.

9. As a final suggestion for this new cinematic form of theater, a small detail of the theater should be taken into account. The advantage the theater has over the cinema is its ephemerality: Once the performance is over, it is gone forever. Even if a theater production is played again and again, it will not be the same production. This is not true in the world of cinema, where films are circulated again and again on screens, on videos, and on television. Such is not the case with the theater. The only consolation the theater has to offer that the cinema does not possess is its program. The cinematic theater should supply its audience with a production program.

Explorations of the Cinematic Theater
and the Cinematic Stage

Many of the previous properties were applied in the productions that are described in this section. Except for *Michi's Blood*, which took place in New York, these productions were carried out by the Experimental Theater Lab (ETL), which was formed in 1990 at Stanford University. The goal of the ETL was to develop and test the principles and properties of the cinematic theater. What follows are brief descriptions of how the elements of cinematic theater were applied in each production, in the hope that this will make the concept more concrete and also suggest possibilities for future exploration. At the beginning of the discussion of each play, the elements of cinematic theater employed in the production are included in a bulleted list.

Fragments of a Revolution by Babak Ebrahimian

- Image/text
- Tableaux/*Gestus*
- The "pregnant moment"
- Cinematic/epic structure
- Sequenced tableaux
- Program with no credits
- No curtain call

This production was based on an epic poem about the 1979 Iranian Revolution, as seen through the eyes of a young boy. The original poem was divided into sections, and each section was numbered and self-contained. To stage these numbered sections of the poem, each fragment was first given a title, and then rendered into a visual tableau with a central *gestus* communicating the title and the heart of the poem. The tableaux were staged using little or no text, and very little music and sound effects. The *text* of the stage, for the most part, consisted of the *visual images*—the *framed tableaux*.

The tableaux all succeeded each other in a linear manner, with no two tableaux linked to one another. Each tableau had its own vignette, its own set of characters, and its own time. For example, while one tableau ("Decadence in the Park") was rapidly paced, another tableau ("Tea") was set to a slow and constant rhythm of a foot tapping against the cold wall of a house. The narrative was structured and presented through a series of tableaux, *sequenced* to create a linear *visual track*.

The production was framed with a prologue, situating the piece historically, and an epilogue that consisted of an excerpt of vocal artist Laurie Anderson's song, *The Dream Before* (1989), dedicated to Walter Benjamin: "History is an angel being blown backwards into the future."
The production had *no curtain call.*

Figure 4.4. Poster image for *Fragments of a Revolution*, 1990.

Hamletmachine by **Heiner Müller**

- The synthetic fragment, or the "deconstructed epic theater"; a "DNA structure" versus epic theater
- A frame for the stage
- *Raum* (space/room): a unified visual aesthetic for the cinematic stage
- A Cartesian plane for blocking
- The sound plane and vertical montage: a sound track for time and sound transitions
- A program with no credits
- No curtain call

The text of Heiner Müller's *Hamletmachine* is largely composed of different threads from history and literary works, all carefully interwoven into a single strand called the *synthetic fragment*.[49] Whereas the epic theater of Bertolt Brecht proceeds in a linear and orderly fashion, through a succession of tableaux, the synthetic fragment is a "deconstructed epic theater"; it exists as a melange of images and quotations. Perhaps a good metaphor for the synthetic fragment is the DNA molecule, which is composed of different strands carefully woven together into a single entity. The silkscreen paintings of Robert Rauschenberg provide another metaphor, in which colors, paintings, text, and images of contemporary history and culture are juxtaposed and combined with each other to yield the final painting.

To have unified visual aesthetics that could contain the synthetic fragment, the space was converted into a *Raum*. Furthermore, the stage design idea was extended to include a *frame* (at the base of the stage) through which the audience could watch the production.[50]

Figure 4.5. Model of the frame for *Hamletmachine*, 1991. Photograph by the author.

As the text was extremely abstract, with little stageable imagery, many of the tableaux served the original text by echoing and mirroring it, rather than duplicating it. (Müller himself had said that the difficult stage images that he has written in his texts are to serve as an inspiration for the director, not as stage directions to be followed in a precise fashion.)

To create these abstract images and blocking with a high degree of precision, the stage was divided into a plane with the four mathematical quadrangles: I, II, II, and IV. Furthermore, to make matters precise, the actors were all given numbers: odd numbers (1, 3, and 5) for the men, and even numbers (2, 4, 6, 8, and 10) for the women. The blocking was then done based on the combination of mathematical drawings on *Cartesian coordinates* and their spatial renditions on the stage. As Müller's text is divided into five sections—five fragments—a primary image was carefully composed for each part.

The next step was to move these sculpted images and bring them to life. Inspired by Robert Wilson's work, the sculpted images were brought to life primarily through *slow motion*. Again, the motion was blocked in space according to the Cartesian coordinates. Each image then had a starting position A and a final position B. The time, *t*, was to be dictated by the vertical montage.

To create atmosphere for the images inside the *Raum*, an additional layer of text was added: *sound + music*. The *sound track* was composed of different pieces of music, sometimes intermixed with sound. Each section had its own texture and music, while certain pieces were used a few times as *theme music* for certain images.

The sound track was created on a standard multitrack system. This enabled the mixing of different pieces of music and sound effects into a single sound track. The sound track was also mixed in such a manner that one theme from a previous section intersected with the theme of the following section, thus creating a *sound carryover* as well as sound cues for the actors. In this mix of themes, sounds, functioning as aural leitmotivs, were also used as a scene partitioning device. The final design of the sound track, which contained music, sound effects, and extra prerecorded music, served as a sound plane structuring the entire performance text. The following is the basic structure of the sound track:

0. Prologue: a line from Laurence Olivier's *Hamlet*,
   intermixed with the sound of the seashore;
   crossfade to:

1. Beethoven, 5th symphony, last movement;
   Philip Glass *Glassworks*, track #5;
   crossfade sound divider into:

2. Philip Glass *Glassworks*, track #1 (Ophelia's Theme);
   crossfade sound divider into:

3. Philip Glass *Glassworks*, track #5, intermixed with
   Tom Waits and sounds of thunder and rain;

4. Philip Glass *Glassworks*, track #3 (choral); *Vocalise* by Rachman-
   inoff intermixed with war sound effects from Kubrick's film *Full
   Metal Jacket*;
   two tracks of music from *Full Metal Jacket*;
   Mark Isham *Film Music*, track #1;
   Mark Isham *Film Music*, track #2;
   crossfade sound divider into:

5. Philip Glass *Glassworks*, track #1 (Ophelia's theme),
   intermixed with the sound of the seashore [closure].

Apart from structuring the performance piece, the sound track created and

dictated an *exact timing* for each of the different tableaux. The actors, for example, knew how to get from their starting position of A [Cartesian coordinates
(x,y,z)] to their final destination $A'(x',y',z')$ based on the sound track. The constant soundtrack, which lasted the one hour and ten minutes of each performance, started the production and carried it through until the end, serving as a
conductor, directing the sculptures through time. All the images were thus created and set in motion through the sound and the process of vertical montage; at
each rehearsal, they were edited and reedited until they matched the sound track
and established a one-to-one correspondence, that is, a *vertical montage*. This
entire process of "sculpting in time" through the vertical montage required an
immense amount of patience, precision, and time.

The production ended with the sound of surf simultaneously cross fading
with house lights fading up. There was no curtain call. The production included
a program with no credits.

The Wedding by Anton Chekhov

- Fragmented and montaged script through the montage of attractions
- Fixed time through the sound track and the vertical montage
- A program *with* credits
- No curtain call

In this production, Chekhov's text was staged, back-to-back, in two different forms: Chekhov I and Chekhov II. While the second version (Chekhov II)
staged the full text of the play in a fairly conventional manner, the first version
(Chekhov I) gave a montaged version of the text. In juxtaposition to the second
version (the full text), Chekhov I stood on its own as a complete production with
a complete narrative.

In Chekhov I, the principle of *montage of attractions* was applied to the
original Chekhov text to yield a new script. The original Chekhov was selec-
tively cut into different segments, and each segment was then further reduced in
the amount of text it contained. Finally, the orders of the scenes were rearranged
and sequenced in such a manner as to create a completely new script.

The script was blocked and staged around a long table. Lighting was
strongly emphasized to fragment and create the necessary cinematic visual effect
for the tableaux. In the first version, which lasted approximately 25 minutes,
there were over 120 light cues. Each cinematic "look" was also precisely defined, sculpted, and dictated by the lighting. As in film, lighting in the theater is
a crucial tool for sculpting in space. Regarding lighting in the cinema, Fellini
remarks:

> Light is the very substance of a film. In film—I have said this before—light is
> ideology, feeling, color, tone, profundity, atmosphere, storytelling. Light is

what adds, cancels out, reduces, exalts, enriches, creates nuances, underlines, alludes to; it makes the fantastic and the dream believable and acceptable or, on the other hand, makes reality fantasy and turns everyday drabness into mirage; it adds transparency, suggests tensions and vibrations. Light excavates a face or smoothes it out, creates expression where none exists, endows dullness with intelligence, makes the insipid seductive. Light outlines the elegance of the body, glorifies a countryside which may be nothing by itself, gives a background magic. Light is the premier special effect, a kind of makeup, a sleight of hand, an enchantment, an alchemist's shop, a mechanism for marvels. Light is the hallucinatory salt which, burning, unleashes visions. Whatever lives on film lives by means of light. The most elementary or crudely made set design can by means of light reveal unexpected perspectives or steep the story in a hushed, brooding atmosphere. Or merely by replacing a powerful light source with shadows, change of light can dissolve a sense of agony and turn everything serene, familiar, reassuring. Films are written in light, their style expressed by means of light.[51]

While the lighting highlighted and sculpted the tableaux in space, the sound track unified the fragments and directed them in time. Based on the sound track, the actors were aware of their next cues. Furthermore, through the *vertical montage* and the usage of a complete, *continuous sound track of music and sounds* (Keith Jarrett, Shostakovich, Pierre Boulez), each scene was linked to the next. In this manner, the vertical montage not only linked, unified, and held the highly fragmented images together, but it also gave the entire performance piece a fixed time, *t*.

The program included the production credits, but as in the previous productions, there were *no curtain calls*.

Michi's Blood by **Franz Xavier Kroetz**

A study in black-and-white film aesthetics and camera point of view:

- Rotating stage ninety degrees to create a variable point of view
- Black-and-white film aesthetics
- Vertical montage, sound effects, and sound environment

Franz Xavier Kroetz's plays are often written as if they were to be performed for television. They have a television sitcom-like structure, with short and rapid scenes. To this end, *Michi's Blood*, a piece with two actors, lends itself very easily to cinematic exploration.

To begin with, as both the space and the set were simple, the set was rotated ninety degrees by the actors themselves. The rotation of the stage was to explore and demonstrate the notion of *(camera) point of view*. In the theater, the stage is usually fixed, and the audience has only one visual perspective. In the cinema, the camera provides a multitude of perspectives by constantly positioning itself at different locations. In this production, the rotation was repeated four times, thus enabling the audience to see the setting with four different points of view.

To link the tableaux to one another during the intervals in which the actors rotated the stage, different television *intermission sounds* were heard, such as the theme music to *Jeopardy*, or a series of dish washing and soap detergent advertisements.

The visuals of the tableaux also implemented a sense of black and white on the stage, by using blue gelled light. As in *The Wedding*, the blue gel helped to shift the color gradient, thereby giving the full *black-and-white effect* on the entire stage, for both the set and costumes. The black-and-white effect was broken in only one tableau: "the morning after," which was lit with an orange gelled light.

The tableaux in this production were, once again, held together by the *vertical montage*: a continuous sound track that included music as well as a complex sound environment, ranging from industrial sounds to the everyday noise of television and a neighbor singing in the upstairs apartment.

The program included both credits as well as curtain call.

City of Refuge by Jean-Marie Apostolidès

A comparative exploration of the *stage realm* and the *cinema realm*:

- Imagination versus reality; film (screen) versus theater (stage)
- The fold: [frame and screened] stage for cinematic theater
- The fold, [frame and screen], also function to separate the film and theater realities
- Behind the fold: a natural built-in *Raum*
- First definition of cinematic theater: perceptual distancing through the fold (*frame + screen*)
- vertical track via speakers
- Kurosawa's montage theory of symphonic structure, or the Noh theater:
- *Introduction, Destruction, Haste.*
- Vertical montage: fixed time; text and music on one level projected from speakers
- Theme music for characters
- Film music exploration: atmospheric music from Wenders' *Wings of Desire* and theme music from Jean-Jacques Beineix's *Betty Blue*
- Cinematic theater movement explorations: Kubrick's counterpoint movement with the music, and Richard Foreman's slow motion with microphoned actor/character
- No curtain call
- Projection of credits onto screen

This production was the first official attempt to explore and define the cinematic theater. Although previous productions had explored film aesthetics and the cinematic stage, none had explicitly tried to replicate and produce a new form of theater. *City of Refuge* was constructed in such a manner that it lent itself perfectly to explorations of theater versus film. The play portrayed an imprisoned man along with his thoughts (imagination, memories, and dreams).

From a dramaturgical and directorial perspective, it seemed appropriate to create a script in which the dichotomy between theater and film was emphasized. The space and reality of a character on stage—all that the man does and says, all the actions that take place, such as his walking, eating, sleeping, and awakening—could be placed in a realm that is *real* and *immediate*, that is, the *theater reality*. On the other hand, all that takes place in his mind—his thoughts, his dreams, his imagination, his memories—are all intangible and not part of the theater reality. If anything, they have a reality of their own, and this reality can then be designated as the realm of *imagination* or *thought,* or the realm of *film.* In this way, the text was shaped into a script that played off of these two realities, film and theater, thereby becoming "cinematic theater."

The logic of the script was then applied to the space of the performance. Downstage, close to the audience, was the immediate and real *space of theater,* and upstage, away from the audience and behind the fold, was the *film space,* or the space of imagination and thought.

The film realm was separated from the theater realm primarily by a two-dimensional line. Designating the two realms as apart from one another, in two dimensions, was the first step. Next, to create two different spaces (in R4 space and time), a fold was created. A separation was made not through a fourth wall, but rather through a frame and a screen; the audience was now to see the film reality through a screen, as if in a cinema. Designating and separating the two spaces with a screened frame created the sense of two enclosed and different spaces. Whereas the audience was seated in the realm of reality—in the theater realm—it witnessed, through the fold, another enclosed, self-contained, autonomous *Raum* with a time of its own. The only spatial element pertaining to the cinematic theater project that unfortunately could not take place was the actual physical distancing of the film realm further away from the audience.

The images within the cinematic theater world were developed and blocked in a highly stylized manner, using Cartesian coordinates. Each image was created independent of the others, and each tableau had its own rhythm, tempo, and texture. Following Kurosawa's suggestion that a good film script should follow a symphonic structure or the Noh theater structure of "introduction, destruction, and haste," the tableaux were sequenced to match the three parts.

Finally, when the space and visuals had been fully sculpted, the tableaux in the film realm were each given a carefully selected piece of music, with an exact length of time. Through this dubbing process, the *vertical montage* process, all the tableaux had a fixed time (t).

The music selection, carefully selected from film music and sound track, served to fill the space with atmosphere for the *Raum* of the cinematic theater. Almost all of the selections were instrumental, solo performances of cello and vocals, or the main instrument themes from the soundtrack. In a few instances, the music for several tableaux was selected to counter the image—*counterpoint*. To enhance the counterpoint, sometimes the action was done in *slow motion*, a technique borrowed from the cinema. Last but not least, the characters in these tableaux each had *theme music*.

The text spoken by the actors in the cinematic theater realm [track 1] was to be amplified through body microphones and simultaneously mixed with music of the tableaux [track 2] to create a single audio track [track 1+2]. Furthermore, the audio track was to be projected through a set of speakers *behind* the audience. Unfortunately, due to the quality of the microphones, this concept was not actualized. Instead, another solution was implemented: The spoken text of the actors was recorded and mixed with the music track. The final sound track then consisted of a single track, and the actors lip-synched their words. The final audio track was projected through speakers behind the audience, as originally intended.

At the end of the play, the theme music faded up and the credits were projected onto the screen. As in the cinema, there was no curtain call.

Fragments of an America by **Babak Ebrahimian**

- Second definition of *cinematic theater*:
  cinematic tableau and spatial distancing
- Cinematic theater and contrasting forms of theater

This production, a self-generated text, was an attempt to look at "America" through a critical lens. In structure, the play was divided into three parts: Part I, Part II, and Part III. Part I consisted of exposés of situations in two theater genres: first through the solo monologue, followed by a cinematic tableau, and then by the exposition of the theme presented in the monologues. Part II was a cabaret with a collage of songs and music by Brecht and Weill from the *Three Penny Opera*. And finally, Part III was a distanced (in space) cinematic tableau portraying "a wedding in the country, in the rain, beside a red wheel barrow," echoing William Carlos Williams image and poem "The Red Wheelbarrow." This third section represented the first attempt at creating a spatially distanced cinematic tableau.

In the previous productions, the cinematic stage and cinematic theater had never been fully distanced in space and from the audience. With *Fragments of an America*, this distancing of the cinematic stage was implemented. Furthermore, cinematic tableaux were generated and created in the script itself.

Depending on the content of the tableau, the cinematic tableaux varied in style: some were realistic, others were stylized and carnivalesque, and still others were hyperreal. As it is important to place the speech and the dialogue at the same level as music and sound in the film sound track, the lack of microphones made it impossible to incorporate the spoken texts into the tableaux. The tableaux were, for the most part, thus created using one or more of the following combinations: (i) a single piece of music; (ii) sounds and sound effects only; (iii) several pieces of music; (iv) music + sound, or (v) several pieces of music + several pieces of sound. Independent of the audio track, the cinematic tableaux were all located at a distance from the audience on a proscenium stage. The timing of the different cinematic tableaux varied both in length as well as in nature; they ranged from a minute to five minutes, and from highly stylized slow-motion action to real time or a quick glance, a simple flash. Each tableau, however, remained constant in its style throughout its fixed time frame (t).

[Whereas the cinematic tableaux and the cinematic stage are essentially one and the same, not all cinematic stages are part of the cinematic theater.] The principles of the cinematic theater requires that the cinematic stage to be contained within the space of a fold + a *Raum* + distancing. The theater in which *Fragment of an Americas* was staged at fortunately had a dressing room directly behind the proscenium stage wall. In reality, this last wall was not a solid wall, but rather consisted of movable blocks. Moving the blocks, at a great distance from the audience—at the end of a long corridor or tunnel—revealed an entire room ready to be used.

This "dressing room" *Raum*—already a "room" and a "space"—was utilized as the space for the last section of this cinematic theater event. Located far away from the audience, the set designers first framed the space from the outside with a constructed frame. Then, along with the lighting designer, they replaced and reconstructed the entire "dressing room" with an outdoor landscape: a small plot of land with a tree, a haystack, and a blue sky. For this outdoor *Raum*, the sound designer created a sound environment consisting of birds softly singing, rain, and the sound of Gershwin's piano Prelude No. 1 in the background. The sum of all the audio and visual elements created a cinematic beauty, which was named *Simple Utopias*. Within this cinematic theater space, a young farm boy with a red wheelbarrow entered and sat down on the haystack. A bride and other members of the community arrived, and a small wedding was held while it rained. During the rainfall, everyone danced in pairs, while holding umbrellas in their hands, and then exited. Only the red wheelbarrow remained on stage, as the lights slowly faded out.

As in the cinema, there was no curtain call.

Credits were projected onto the screen.

Notes

1. Liviu Ciulei, in discussion with the author, 1995.

2. I would like to emphasize that bringing the theater into the cinema is not unique to Orson Welles. Welles' usage of the theater was unique in that he framed the scene, and thus created a [framed theater]. Other directors, most notably Federico Fellini, use the theater in the cinema, in different ways. For example, take the later films of Fellini. In each and every one, Fellini designs and creates an entire set for them. For example, the brightly colored sea, realistic yet fantastical, that one sees in *Amarcord* is all synthetic, made from a plastic sheet, with stagehands moving it and corrected lighting. The same holds true for the sea and the rhinoceros at the end of *And the Ship Sails On*, and the gigantic sets of *Satyricon* and *City of Women*. They all had to be built from scratch. There is no need to take the camera to the location when you can create a better one, on stage, in the studio—even for natural things such as the daylight. Fellini writes:

> I believe in light, and light is what I use, what my imagination needs. My light will never be sunlight. I believe in constructing daylight, and even the sea in the studio. In *Amarcord*, I built the sea. And nothing is truer than that sea on the screen. It is the sea I wanted, which the real sea would never have given me. How do you build the sea? That's a trade secret I would not want to reveal. A couple of sheets of plastic and a couple of good-natured operators, and you have it. I work for this, to be there, to cut and nail, paint and set up lights. The cinema is an illusion: an image that must emerge for what it is.

Frederico Fellini, "The birth of a film," in *Fellini on Fellini*, eds. Anna Keel and Christian Strich, trans. Isabel Quigley (New York: Dell Publishing Company, Inc., 1976), 165.

3. Bazin, André, *Orson Welles*, trans. Jonathan Rosenbaum (New York: Harper & Row, 1978), 45.

4. Bazin, *Orson Welles*, 38.

5. Bazin, *Orson Welles*, 47.

6. See Bazin, *Orson Welles*, 48. Here, Bazin gives a most vivid description of the impact of this radio-theatrical event—an impact well worth noting, due to the contagious panic it caused among the masses:

> The rest is history, and if the event hadn't left tangible traces and became the object of serious scientific studies, we would scarcely believe today that it happened, especially on such a scale. This extraordinary phenomenon of collective, nationwide schizophrenia would seem to be an inflated publicity gimmick or a figment of the Welles legend. But the facts are inescapable. An unidentified announcer broke in during the broadcast with prime news of the landing of the Martians in New Jersey; then from time to time, other communications of this sort, including a "dramatic" speech from the Secretary of the Interior; finally the President came on to confirm the gravity of the situation. [Bazin is in error on this detail regarding the President.] This was all it took for thousands, then hundreds of thousands and finally millions of listeners to believe that the end of the world had come. The consequences of this panic are celebrated: people fled

in all directions, those from the city to the country and vice versa. In the dead of night, highways were streaked with innumerable cars. Priests were called to hear confessions. There were miscarriages, broken limbs in the scuffles, heart attacks; hospital and psychiatric centers didn't know how to cope with the rush of patients. In Pittsburgh, a woman took her own life rather than let herself be violated by the Martians. In the South, people prayed together in public places. Looting began in half-abandoned cities. In New Jersey, the National Guard was called out. Several days—if not several weeks—later, Red Cross Volunteers and Quakers were still going up into the Black Hills of Dakota, persuading the miserable, terrorized families that they could return to their homes. Along with Orson Welles, there was undoubtedly at least one beneficiary of this collective hysteria—the worthy Mr. Hadley Cantril, professor of psycho-sociology at Princeton University, who took delight in this subject and described it in a learned work as the "first modern panic that has been studied with the research tools now available to the social scientist."

7. The filmmaking industry is run and governed by the producers. In "Chambre 666," a group of directors give their views on the condition of and future of cinema. Steven Spielberg makes the following statement regarding Hollywood and the producers of current-day films:

It appears that everyone in positions of power in Hollywood—those people in the studios with the power to say yes or no—wants a hit. They want an unstoppable thunderbolt in extra time in the final of the World Cup, with the score at four-all. Everyone wants to be a hero, and just before lights-out in Hollywood they want to take a piece of shit out of their desk drawer and turn it into a silk purse, and produce a last-minute hit, a $100 million hit. The studio bosses seem to think that if a film doesn't promise to be at least a hit, preferably a blockbuster, they want to have nothing to do with it.

Wim Wenders, *The Logic of Images: Essays and Conversations*, trans. Michael Hofmann (London: Faber and Faber, 1991), 30.

To continue to demonstrate the extent of the commercialization of the film industry (Hollywood) in America, observe the following remark from Fellini about the aftermath of *La Strada*:

After *La Strada* I had scores of offers. To make *Il bidone*, which I was then planning? No. To make *Gelsomina on a Bicycle* or anything with Gelsomina in the title. They didn't realize that in *La Strada* I had already said all I wanted to say about Gelsomina. They all wanted Gelsomina. I could have earned a fortune selling her name to a doll manufacturers, to sweet firms; even Walt Disney wanted to make an animated cartoon about her. I could have lived on Gelsomina for twenty years!

Frederico Fellini, "The bitter life—of money," in *Fellini on Fellini*, eds. Anna Keel and Christian Strich, trans. Isabel Quigley (New York: Dell Publishing Company, Inc., 1976), 88.

As for the role of the producers and their control over the artistic aspects of the film, Fellini makes an observation that still holds true today, and with his observation, he proposes the ideal dream of every filmmaker:

> I know what it means for a young director to fight against the despotism of the producers. . . . If I had to give a definition of the policy of my company, I would say that it is one that will never make its directors change the endings of their films. Producers always want to change the endings. I shall leave the director to do as he wishes. Rizzoli has faith in me. I shall have faith in my directors.

Fellini, "The bitter life—of money," 89–90.

Complete freedom is what every director dreams of, and complete freedom is what every film director lacks. Regarding his lifelong career as a filmmaker, Ingmar Bergman makes the following observation: "Today, I feel that in *Persona*—and later in *Cries and Whispers*—I had gone as far as I could go. And in these two instances, when working in total freedom, I touched wordless secrets that only the cinema can discover." Bergman, *Images: My Life in Film*, 65.

8. Welles' first choice was to adapt Joseph Conrad's *Heart of Darkness*, with himself as the adapter, the director, and actor, playing the roles of both Marlow and Kurtz. The production fell through when the war broke out. The next project, a thriller film entitled *The Smiler with a Knife*, was also abandoned because the stars who were asked to play the roles did not want to risk working with a young, inexperienced genius. The third and last project was then *Citizen Kane*, conceived and written by Orson Welles and Herman J. Mankiewicz.

9. At a very young age, Welles made a short black-and-white silent film mocking the avant-garde tradition, but this film was more for fun than anything else.

10. Due to the war, the film opened in France six years later. The film had an enormous impact on the cinema scene, especially on the young generation of directors who were surprised by Welles' young age. François Truffaut remarks: "I rather think that this unusual first name contributed to our fascination: Orson sounded like *ourson*, a bear cub, and we heard that this cub was only thirty, that he'd made *Citizen Kane* at twenty-six, the same age at which Eisenstein had made *Potemkin*." François Truffaut, *The Films in My Life*, trans. Leonard Mayhew (New York: Simon and Schuster, 1978), 277. Although Welles and Eisenstein were the same age, *Potemkin* was Eisenstein's third film, not his first.

11. In 2002, 250 directors and critics were asked to give their top 10 choices of films, and top 10 choices of directors. The results were as follows:

Critics' top 10 films:
1. *Citizen Kane* (Welles 1941)
2. *Vertigo* (Hitchcock 1958)
3. *La Regle du jeu* (Renoir 1939)
4. *The Godfather* and *The Godfather Part II* (Coppola 1972, 1974)
5. *Tokyo Story* (Ozu 1953)

Directors' top 10 films:
1. *Citizen Kane* (Welles 1941)
2. *The Godfather* and *The Godfather Part II* (Coppola, 1972, 1974)
3. *8 1/2* (Fellini 1963)
4. *Lawrence of Arabia* (Lean 1962)
5. *Dr. Strangelove* (Kubrick 1963)

6. *2001: A Space Odyssey*
   (Kubrick 1968)
7. *Battleship Potemkin* (Eisenstein 1925)
8. *Sunrise* (Murnau 1927)
9. *81/2* (Fellini 1963)
10. *Singin'in the Rain* (Kelly, Donen
    1951)

6. *The Bicycle Thief* (De Sica 1948)
   Raging Bull (Scorsese 1980)
   Vertigo (Hitchcock 1958)
9. *Rashomon* (Kurosawa 1950)
   La Regle du jeu (Renoir 1939)
   Seven Samurai (Kurosawa 1954)

Critics' Top 10 Directors:
1. Welles
   Hitchcock
3. Godard
4. Renoir
5. Kubrick
6. Kurosawa
7. Fellini
8. Ford
9. Eisenstein
10. Coppola
    Ozu

Directors' top 10 Directors:
1. Fellini
2. Welles
3. Kurosawa
4. Coppola
5. Hitchcock
6. Kubrick
7. Wilder
8. Bergman
9. Scorsese
   Lean
   Renoir

Sight & Sound magazine, 12, no. 9 (September 2002): 24.

12. Bazin, *Orson Welles*, 76.

13. Bazin, *Orson Welles*, 59.

14. Today, films receive Academy Awards a dime a dozen for best actor, best director, best screenplay, etc.; *Titanic* (1997) won eleven academy awards, *The English Patient* (1996) won six, and *Shakespeare in Love* (1998) won five. In contrast, *Citizen Kane* only received one Academy Award—for the best screenplay.

15. Truffaut, *The Films in My Life*, 281–282.

16. Richard France, "Citizen Will," *American Theater* 5, no. 7 (October 1988): 107.

17. Bazin, *Orson Welles*, 13.

20. Truffaut, *The Films in My Life*, 282. In my opinion, however, Welles fully exploited and took sound usage to its height with his film *The Trial*, based on Kafka's novel. I believe that *The Trial*—despite the fact that Welles did not endorse it as one of his finest films—is in fact on par with *Citizen Kane*, and in terms of its music and sound usage, it is perhaps even superior. In this film, Welles does not let go of the sound track for even a split second. Furthermore, his usage of music, in addition to sound and text, is extremely diverse and versatile, ranging from jazz to Albinoni's *Adagio*.

19. Truffaut, *The Films in My Life*, 282.

20. Bazin, *Orson Welles*, 74.

21. François Truffaut, "Foreword," in *Orson Welles*, ed. André Bazin, trans. Jonathan Rosenbaum (New York: Harper & Row, 1978), 7.

22. Truffaut, "Foreword," Truffaut notes that *Citizen Kane* runs exactly one hour and fifty-nine minutes. This exactitude of timing, maintains Truffaut, is a task that Welles learned from his radio days. "The whole problem for the film-maker—no, not the whole problem but a substantial part of it—is to learn how to come to grips with running time. In many films, the expositional scenes are too long, the "privileged" scenes too short, which winds up equalizing everything and leads to rhythmic monotony. Here we can say

that Welles benefited from his experience as a radio storyteller, for he must have had to learn to differentiate sharply between expositional scenes (reduced to flashes of four to eight seconds) and genuine emotional scenes of three to four minutes."

23. Truffaut, "Foreword," 10.

24. Truffaut, "Foreword," 10.

25. Bazin, *Orson Welles*, 27.

26. Liviu Ciulei, in discussion with the author, 1995.

27. I owe this observation regarding focus on stage to Carl Weber.

28. Truffaut, "Foreword," 11.

29. Bazin, *Orson Welles*, 73.

30. Bazin, *Orson Welles*, 68.

31. Bazin, *Orson Welles*, 68.

32. To be precise, the shot runs 4:25 with one pan in the beginning and one pan at the end.

33. Bazin, *Orson Welles*, 72.

34. See Mankiewicz and Welles, "The Shooting Script" 257.

35. My own *mise-en-scène* of the scene.

36. The difference between a shooting script and a continuity script lies in the before and after. The shooting script is the working script that the writer/director create upon which to base their shooting. The continuity script is the final script as taken directly from the fully edited final film.

37. See Mankiewicz and Welles, "The Shooting Script," 405.

38. Bazin, *Orson Welles*, 77–78.

39. Bazin, *Orson Welles*, 78.

40. Wenders, *The Logic of Images*, 4.

43. In Frank Beaver, ed., *Dictionary of Film Terms: The Aesthetic Companion to Film Analysis* (New York: Twayne Publishers, 1994), 271–272, Pan (or Panning) is defined as follows:

> The movement of the camera across a scene horizontally (left to right or right to left) while mounted on a fixed base. The pan, like the tilt, is frequently used to scan a scene and to follow character movement in a limited location. Establishing shots often include pans, and sometimes tilts, to provide a more extensive view of an environment. In character movement, the camera can pan to follow an actor's walk across a room and then tilt down when the actor sinks into an easy chair.
>
> Pans and tilts, while for the most part utilitarian, allow the director to present a scene or follow actions fully without edits that might destroy a desired mood.
>
> Rapidly effected pans are also often used dynamically to reveal character reactions or to reveal and emphasize important information ("revelation pans"). Pans can also be incorporated into subjective shots as the camera assumes the point of view of a character and surveys a room or exterior location. The use of pans and tilts in this way makes the subjective, mind's eye point of view more obvious by activating the camera. An extremely rapid pan, referred to as a swish pan, is a method of effecting a transition from one scene to another. The rapid swish pan blurs the image, thus wiping out the scene. A new scene then begins.

42. Interestingly enough, Sokurov filmed *The Russian Ark*, in one continuous take of 90 minutes, but then due to the complicated shooting, he, much like Fellini, dubbed the sound and added the sound track after the shooting.

43. Truffaut, *The Films in My Life*, 283–284.

44. Bazin, *Orson Welles*, 21.

45. Bazin, *Orson Welles*, 109.

46. Bazin, *Orson Welles*, 16–17.

47. Bazin, *Orson Welles*, 17.

48. Bazin, *Orson Welles*, 111.

49. See Chapter 1, note 34.

50. Due to technical difficulties and fire regulations, this aspect of the design, the frame, was not implemented. It was, however, tried in a later production, *Fragments of an America*.

51. Federico Fellini, *Comments on Film*, ed. Giovanni Grazzini, trans. Joseph Henry. (Fresno, Ca.: Press at California State University, 1988), 154–157.

Bibliography

Anderson, Laurie. *Empty Places: A Performance*. New York: Harper Perennial, 1991.

Arnheim, Rudolf. *Film as Art*. London: Faber and Faber, 1958.

———. *Visual Thinking*. Berkeley: University of California Press, 1969.

Artaud, Antonin. *Oeuvres Complètes*. Tomes I–IX. Paris: Éditions Gallimard, 1964–1979.

———. *Selected Writings*. Edited by Susan Sontag. Translated by Helen Weaver. Berkeley: University of California Press, 1976.

———. *Theatre and Its Double*. Translated by Mary Caroline Richards. New York: Grove Press, 1958.

———. *Theatre et Son Double*. Paris: Éditions Gallimard, 1964.

Aumont, Jacques. *Montage/Eisenstein*. Translated by Lee Hildreth, Constance Penley, and Andrew Ross. Bloomington: Indiana University Press, 1987.

Bachelard, Gaston. *The Poetics of Space*. Translated by Maria Jolas. Boston: Beacon Press, 1994.

Barba, Eugenio, and Nichola Savarese. *Dictionary of Theatre Anthropology: The Secret Art of the Performer*. Translated by Richard Fowler. London: Routledge, 1991.

Barthes, Roland. *A Barthes Reader*. Edited by Susan Sontag. New York: Noonday Press, 1982.

———. *Camera Lucida: Reflections on Photography*. Translated by Richard Howard. New York: Hill and Wang, 1981.

———. *Critical Essays*. Translated by Richard Howard. Evanston, Ill.: Northwestern University Press, 1972.

———. *The Grain of Voice: Interviews 1962–1980*. Translated by Linda Coverdale. New York: Hill and Wang, 1985.

———. *Oeuvres Complètes*. Tomes I–II. Edited by Eric Morty. Paris: Éditions du Seuil, 1993–1994.

———. *The Responsibility of Forms: Critical Essays on Music, Art, and Representation*. Translated by Richard Howard. New York: Hill and Wang, 1985.

Baudrillard, Jean. *America*. Translated by Chris Turner. London: Verso, 1988.

———. *Selected Writings*. Edited by Mark Poster. Stanford, Calif.: Stanford

University Press, 1988.

———. *Simulations*. Translated by Paul Foss et al. New York: Semiotexte, 1983.

Bazin, André. *What Is Cinema?* Foreword by Jean Renoir. Translated by Hugh Gray. Berkeley, Calif.: University of California Press, 1967.

———. *Orson Welles*. Forword by François Truffaut. Translated by Jonathan Rosenbaum. New York: Harper & Row, 1978.

Beaver, Frank. *Dictionary of Film Terms: The Aesthetic Companion to Film Analysis*. New York: Twayne Publishers, 1994.

Benjamin, Walter. *Reflections*. Translated by Edmund Jephcott. New York: Schocken Books, 1986.

———. *Illuminations*. Edited by Hannah Arendt. Translated by Harry Zohn. New York: Schocken Books, 1969.

Bergman, Ingmar. *Bergman on Bergman*. London: Secker and Warburg, 1973.

———. *Images: My Life in Film*. Translated by Marianne Ruth. New York: Arcade Publishing, 1994.

———. *The Magic Lantern*. Translated by Joan Tate. New York: Viking, 1988.

Blau, Herbert. *The Audience*. Baltimore: Johns Hopkins University Press, 1990.

Bondy, Luc, and Jurgen Flinm. *Erich Wonder: Stage Design*. Edited by Koschk Hetzer-Molden. Ostfidern, Germany: Hatje Cantz Publishers, 2001.

Boujut, Michel. *Wim Wenders*. Paris: Edilig, 1986.

Bradby, David and David Williams. *Director's Theatre*. London: Macmillan Publishers, 1988.

Braun, Edward. *The Theatre of Meyerhold: A Revolution on the Modern Stage*. New York: Drama Book Specialists, 1979.

Brecht, Bertolt. *Brecht on Theatre*. Translated and edited by John Willett. New York: Hill and Wang, 1964.

———. *Collected Plays*. 9 vols. Translated by John Willett and Ralph Mannheim. New York: Pantheon Books, 1970–77.

———. *Letters 1913–1956*. Edited by John Willett. Translated by Ralph Manheim. New York: Routledge, 1981.

———. *Plays. The Resistible Rise of Arturo Ui. Caucasian Chalk Circle*. Translated by John Willett. New York: Arcade Publishers, 1994.

———. *Poems*. Translated by John Willett and Ralph Mannheim. London: Methuen, 1979.

Brook, Peter. *The Empty Space*. New York: Atheneum, 1968.

———. *The Shifting Point*. New York: Harper & Row, 1987.

———. *The Open Door: Thoughts on Acting and Theatre*. New York: Pantheon Books, 1993.

Brustein, Robert. *The Theatre of Revolt: Studies in Ibsen, Strindberg, Chekhov, Shaw, Brecht, Pirandello, O'Neill, and Genet*. Boston: Little, Brown and Co., 1964.

———. *Who Needs Theatre: Dramatic Opinions*. New York: Atlantic Monthly Press, 1987.

Bürger, Peter. *Theory of the Avant-Garde.* Translated by Michael Shaw. Minneapolis: University of Minnesota Press, 1984.

Cage, John. *Silence.* Middletown, Mass.: Wesleyan University Press, 1962.

Carlson, Marvin. *Theories of the Theatre: A Historical and Critical Survey from the Greeks to the Present.* Ithaca, N.Y.: Cornell University Press, 1984.

―――. *Places of Performance.* Ithaca, N.Y.: Cornell University Press, 1989.

―――. *Theatre Semiotics.* Bloomington: Indiana University Press, 1990.

Carroll, David. *Paraesthetics.* New York: Methuen, 1987.

Clifford, James. *The Predicament of Culture: Twentieth Century Ethnography, Literature, and Art.* Cambridge, Mass.: Harvard University Press, 1988.

Cohen, Robert, and John Harrop. *Creative Play Direction.* Englewood Cliffs, N.J.: Prentice Hall, 1974.

Cole, Toby, and Helen Krich Chinoy, eds. *Directors on Directing: A Source Book of the Modern Theatre.* Indianapolis, Ind.: Bobbs-Merrill Educational Publishing, 1976.

Connor, Steven. *Postmodern Culture: An Introduction to Theories of the Contemporary.* Oxford: Blackwell, 1989.

Cook, David A. *A History of Narrative Film, 3rd Edition.* New York: W.W. Norton & Company, 1996.

Cooper, Anthony, Earl of Shaftsbury. *Second Characters.* Edited by Benjamin Rand. Cambridge, U.K.: Cambridge University Press, 1914.

Culler, Jonathan. *Ferdinand de Saussure.* Ithaca, N.Y.: Cornell University Press, 1986.

―――. *The Pursuit of Signs: Semiotics, Literature, and Deconstruction.* Ithaca, N.Y.: Cornell University Press, 1981.

―――. *On Deconstruction: Theory and Criticism after Structuralism.* Ithaca, N.Y.: Cornell University Press, 1982.

Deleuze, Gilles. *Cinema I: L'Image-Mouvement.* Paris: Les Editions de Minuit, 1983.

―――. *The Fold: Leibniz and the Baroque,* Translated by Tom Conley. Minneapolis: University of Minnesota Press, 1993.

Derrida, Jacques. *Writing and Difference.* Translated by Alan Bass. Chicago: University of Chicago Press, 1978.

―――. *Truth in Painting.* Translated by Geoff Bennington and Ian McLeod. Chicago: University of Chicago Press, 1987.

Diderot, Denis. *Correspondance.* Edited by Georges Roth. Paris: Les Editions de Minuit, 1956.

―――. *Diderot's Writing on the Theatre.* Edited by F.C. Green, New York: AMS Press, 1978.

―――. *Oeuvres Esthétiques.* Edited by Paul Vernière. Paris: Editions Garnier Frères, 1965.

―――. *Paradox sur le comédien.* Paris: Armand Colin, 1992.

―――. *The Paradox of Acting.* Translated by Walter Herries Pollock. New York: Hill and Wang, 1957.

Eco, Umberto. *Semiotics and the Philosophy of Language.* Bloomington: Indiana University Press, 1984.

———. *A Theory of Semiotics.* Bloomington: Indiana University Press, 1976.

Eisenstein, Sergei. *Immoral Memories.* Translated by Herbert Marshall. Boston: Houghton Mifflin Co., 1983.

———. *Film Essays and a Lecture.* Edited and translated by Jay Leyda. New York: Praeger Publishers, Inc. 1970.

———. *Film Form and Film Sense.* Translated by Jay Leyda. Cleveland, Oh.: World Publishing Company, 1957.

———. *Notes of a Film Director.* Translated by X. Danko. London: Lawrence and Wishart, 1959.

Elam, Keir. *The Semiotics of Theatre and Drama.* London: Methuen, 1980.

Esslin, Martin. *The Field of Drama: How the Signs of Drama Create Meaning on Stage and Screen.* London and New York: Methuen, 1987.

———. *The Theatre of the Absurd.* New York: Penguin Books, 1961.

Fellini, Federico. *Fellini on Fellini.* Edited by Anna Keel and Christian Strich. Translated by Isabel Quigley. New York: Delta Books, 1976.

———. *Comments on Film.* Edited by Giovanni Grazzini. Translated by Joseph Henry. Fresno, Calif.: The Press at California State University, 1988.

———. *Propos.* Paris: Editions Buchet/Chastel, 1980.

———. *La Strada.* Edited by Peter Bondanella and Manuela Gieri. New Brunswick, N.J.: Rutgers University, 1987.

Fellows, Otis, ed. *Diderot Studies VII.* Geneva: Librarie Droz, 1965.

———. *Un Regista a Cinecitta.* Milano: Arnoldo Mondadori Editore, 1988.

Foreman, Richard. *Love and Science Selected Music—Theatre Texts.* New York: TCG, 1991.

———. *Unbalancing Acts: Foundations for a Theatre.* New York: TCG, 1992.

Foster, Hal, ed. *The Anti-Aesthetic: Essays on Postmodern Culture.* Port Townsend, Wash.: Bay Press, 1983.

Foucault, Michel. *Discipline and Punish: The Birth of the Prison.* Translated by Alan Sheridan. New York: Vintage Books, 1977.

France, Richard. "Citizen Will," *American Theater* 5, no. 7 (October 1988): 107.

Fried, Michael. *Absorption and Theatricality.* Chicago and London: University of Chicago Press, 1980.

Girard, René. *Shakespeare: A Theatre of Envy.* Oxford: Oxford University, 1991.

Godard, Jean-Luc. *Godard on Godard.* Translated by Martin Secker. New York: The Viking Press, 1972.

Goutier, Henri. *L'essence du Théâtre.* Paris: Librairie Plon, Imprimeurs-Editeurs, 1943.

Grossvogel, David. *The Blasphemers: The Theatre of Brecht, Ionesco, Beckett, and Genet.* Ithaca, N.Y.: Cornell University Press, 1962.

Grotowski, Jerzy. *Towards a Poor Theatre.* Edited by Eugenio Barba. London: Methuen, 1968.

Hartnoll, Phyllis. *The Theatre: A Concise History*. New York: Thomas and Hudson, 1985.

Hassan, Ihab. *The Postmodern Turn*. Columbus: Ohio State Press, 1987.

Hays, David. *Light on the Subject*. New York: Limelight Editions, 1989.

Hays, Michael. *Critical Conditions*. Minneapolis: University of Minnesota Press, 1992.

———. *The Public and Performance*. Ann Arbor: University of Michigan Research Press, 1981.

Hoghe, Raimund. *Pina Bausch: Histoires de Théâtre Dansé*. Translated from German to French by Dominique Petit. Paris: L'Arche, 1987.

Huyssen, Andreas. *After the Great Divide: Modernism, Mass Culture, Postmodernism*. Bloomington: Indiana University Press, 1986.

Ingari, Enzo. *Bertolucci by Bertolucci*. Translated by Donald Ranvaud. London: Plexus, 1987.

Jameson, Fredric. *Postmodernism or the Cultural Logic of Late Capitalism*. Durham: Duke University Press, 1991.

Jones, David Richard. *Great Directors at Work: Stanislavsky, Brecht, Kazan, Brook*. Berkeley: University of California Press, 1986.

Kagan, Norman. *The Cinema of Stanley Kubrick*. New York: Grove Press, Inc. 1972.

Kant, Immanuel. *The Critique of Judgement*. Translated by James Creed Meredith. Oxford: Clarendon Press, 1952.

Kott, Jan. *Shakespeare Our Contemporary*. Translated by Boleslaw Taborski. New York: W.W. Norton and Company, 1974.

———. *The Theatre of Essence*. Evanston, Ill.: Northwestern University Press, 1964.

Kurosawa, Akira. *Something Like an Autobiography*. Translated by Audie E. Bock. New York: Vintage Books Edition, 1983.

Leach, Robert. *Vsevolod Meyerhold*. Cambridge, U.K.: Cambridge University Press, 1989.

Leacroft, Richard and Helen. *Theatre and Playhouse: An Illustrated Survey of Theatre Buildings from Ancient Greece to the Present Day*. London: Methuen, 1984.

Long, Robert Emmet. *Ingmar Bergman: Film and Stage*. New York: Harry N. Abrams, Inc., 1994.

Lyotard, Jean-Françoise. *The Postmodern Condition: A Report on Knowledge*. Translated by George Bennington and Brian Massumi. Minneapolis: University of Michigan Press, 1984.

Macksey, Richard, and Eugenio Donato, eds. *The Structuralist Controversy*. Baltimore: Johns Hopkins University Press, 1970.

Mankiewicz, Herman J., and Orson Welles. *The Citizen Kane Book*. New York: Limelight Editions, 1984.

Marowitz, Charles. *Prospero's Staff*. Bloomington: Indiana University Press, 1986.

Marranca, Bonnie. *The Theatre of Images*. New York: Drama Book Specialists,

1977.

Mason, John Hope. *The Irresistible Diderot*. London, New York: Quartet Books, 1982.

Martin, Carol, and Henry Bial. *Brecht Sourcebook*. New York: Routledge, 2000.

Mast, Gerald. *A Short History of the Movies*. Chicago: The University of Chicago Press, 1981.

Mast, Gerald, and Marshall Cohen. *Film Theory and Criticism*. New York: Oxford University Press, 1985.

Metz, Christian. *Film Language: A Semiotics of Cinema*. Translated by Michael Taylor. New York: Oxford University Press, 1979.

Mitchell, W. J. T. *Iconology: Image, Text, Ideology*. Chicago: The University of Chicago Press, 1986.

Müller, Heiner. *The Battle: Plays, Prose, Poems*. Edited and translated by Carl Weber. New York: PAJ Publications, 1989.

———. *Ciment: Suivi de La Correction*. Translated from German to French by Jean-Pierre Morel. Paris: Les Editions de Minuit, 1991.

———. *Explosions of a Memory*. Edited and translated by Carl Weber. New York: PAJ Publications, 1989.

———. *Fautes d'impression: Textes et Entretiens*. Edited by Jean Jourdheuil. Translated from German to French by Anne Bérélowitch, Jean-Pierre Morel, Jean-François Peyret, Bernard Sobel, and Bernard Umbrecht. Paris: L'Arche, 1991.

———. *Germania*. Translated and annotated by Bernard and Caroline Schütze. Edited by Slyère Lotringer. New York: Semiotext[e], 1990.

———. *Hamletmachine and Other Texts for the Stage*. Edited and translated by Carl Weber. New York: PAJ Publications, 1984.

———. *A Heiner Müller Reader*. Edited and translated by Carl Weber. Baltimore: Johns Hopkins University Press, 2001.

Nagler, A. M. *A Sourcebook in Theatrical History*. New York: Dover Publications Inc., 1952.

Oida, Yahi. *An Actor Adrift*. London: Methuen, 1992.

Palmer, R., ed. *The Cinematic Text: Methods and Approaches*. New York: AMS Press, 1989.

Panofsky, Erwin. *Perspective as Symbolic Form*. Translated by Christopher S. Wood. New York: Zone Books, 1997.

Pavis, Patrice. *Languages of the Stage: Essays in the Semiology of the Theatre*. New York: PAJ Publications, 1982.

———. *Theatre at the Crossroads of Culture*. Translated by Loren Kruger. London: 1992.

Perloff, Marjorie. *The Futurist Movement: Avant Garde, Avant Guerre, and the Language of Rupture*. Chicago: The University of Chicago Press, 1986.

———. *The Poetics of Indeterminacy: Rimbaud to Cage*. Evanston, Ill. : Northwestern University Press, 1999.

———. *Radical Artifice*. Chicago: University of Chicago Press, 1991.

———. *21ˢᵗ-Century Modernism: The "New" Poetics*. Oxford: Blackwell Publishersß, 2002.

Quadri, Franco, Franco Bertoni, and Robert Stearns. *Robert Wilson*. New York: Rizzoli, 1998.

Rabkin, Gerald, ed. *Richard Foreman: Art+Performance*. Baltimore: Johns Hopkins University Press, 1999.

Riddell, Richard. "The German *Raum*," *The Drama Review* 24, no. 1 (March 1980): 39–52.

Robinson, David. *The History of the World Cinema*. New York: Stein and Day, 1973.

Rosen, Philip, ed. *Narrative, Apparatus, Ideology: A Film Theory Reader*. New York: Columbia University Press, 1986.

Russell, Douglas A. *Period Styles for the Theatre*. Boston: Allyn and Bacon Inc., 1980.

Schechner, Richard. *Performance Theory*. New York: Routledge, 1988.

Scorsese Martin. *Scorsese on Scorsese*. London: Faber and Faber, 1989.

Serban, Andrei. "Life as a Sound." *The Drama Review* 72, (1976): 25–26.

Shyer, Laurence. *Robert Wilson and His Collaborators*. New York: TCG, 1989.

Smith, A.C.H. *Orghast At Persepolis*. New York: Viking Press, 1972.

Sontag, Susan. *A Susan Sontag Reader*. New York: Vintage Books, 1983.

Spolin, Viola. *Improvisation for the Theatre: A Handbook of Teaching and Directing Techniques*. Evanston, Ill.: Northwestern University Press, 1983.

Stam, Robert, Robert Burgoyne, and Sandy Flitterman-Lewis. *New Vocabularies in Film Semiotics: Structuralism, Poststructuralism, and Beyond*. London: Routledge, 1992.

Stearns, Robert, and Craig Nelson. *Robert Wilson*. New York: Harper & Row, 1991.

Suzuki, Tadashi. *The Way of Acting: The Theatre Writings of Tadashi Suzuki*. Translated by I. Thomas. New York: Rimer, 1986.

Szondi, Peter. *Theory and Practice of Modern Drama*. Translated by Michael Hays. Minneapolis: University of Minnesota Press, 1986.

Tarkovsky, Andrey. *Sculpting in Time: Reflections on Cinema*. Translated by Kitty Hunter-Blair. New York: Alfred Knopf, 1987.

Tornabene, Francesco. *Federico Fellini: The Fantastic Visions of a Realist*. Translated by Melanie Richter-Beruburg. Berlin: Benedikt Taschen Verlag GmbH, 1990.

Truffaut, François. *The Films in My Life*. Translated by Leonard Mayhew. New York: Simon and Schuster, 1978.

Tschumi, Bernard, ed. *D: The Columbia Documents of Architecture and Theory*. 2 vols. New York: Columbia University Graduate School of Architecture, Planning, and Preservation, 1993.

———. *Architecture and Disjunction*. Cambridge, Mass.: MIT Press, 1994.

Wallis, Brian, ed. *Art after Modernism: Rethinking Representation*. New York: The New Museum of Contemporary Art, 1984.

136   Bibliography

Wenders, Wim. *The Logic of Images: Essays and Conversations.* Translated by Michael Hoffmann. London: Faber and Faber, 1991.

———. *Emotion Pictures.* Translated by Sean Whiteside with Michael Hoffmann. London: Faber and Faber, 1989.

———. *On Film.* London: Faber and Faber, 2001.

———. *Once: Pictures and Stories.* Translated by Marion Kagerer. New York: Distributed Art Publishers, 2001.

Whitmore, Jon. *Directing Postmodern Theatre: Shaping Signification in Performance.* Ann Arbor: University of Michigan Press, 1994.

Wonder, Erich. *Raum-Szenen/Szenen-Raum.* Ostfidern, Germany: Hatje Cantz Publishers, 1986.

Wright, Elizabeth. *Postmodern Brecht: A Re-presentation.* New York and London: Routledge, 1989.

Index

About the Author

Babak Ebrahimian is a theater director, filmmaker, and scholar in New York City. He founded the Experimental Theater Lab at Stanford University, where he developed the key elements of the cinematic theater. His experimental theater productions include both original pieces and works by Chekhov, Brecht, and Heiner Müller, among others. Film credits include *The Voyage* and *The Last Goodbye*. He has taught cinema, theater, and literature at Columbia and Stanford universities, and his articles have been published in *Theatre Journal* and *PAJ: A Journal of Performance and Art*. He holds a Ph.D. and a Masters Degree in Directing from Stanford University. Currently, he is a lecturer at Columbia University.